# Bread for Breakfast

# BREAD FOR BREAKFAST

**Beth Hensperger**

Photography by Leigh Beisch

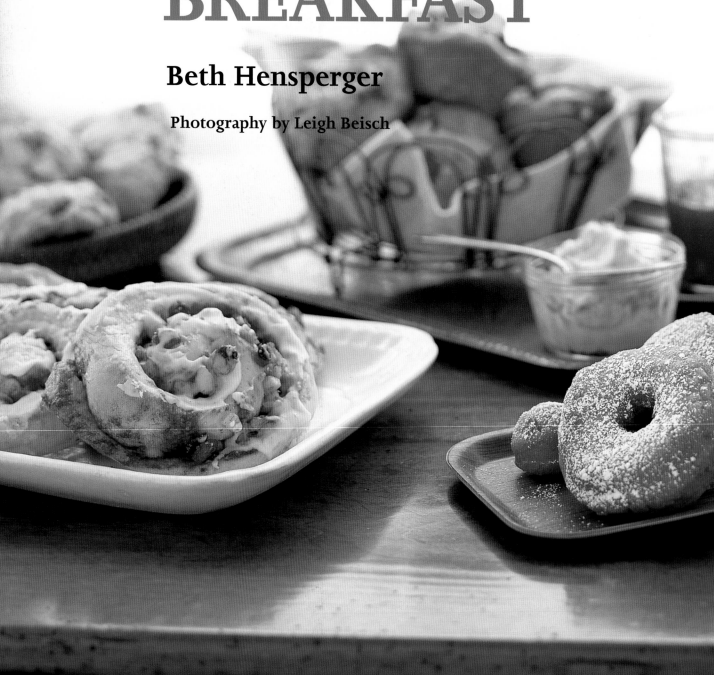

10

TEN SPEED PRESS
Berkeley / Toronto
www.tenspeed.com

# Acknowledgments

Ten Speed Press
P.O. Box 7123
Berkeley, California 94707
www.tenspeed.com

Distributed in Australia by Simon & Schuster
Australia, in Canada by Ten Speed Press Canada,
in New Zealand by Southern Publishers Group, in
South Africa by Real Books, in Southeast Asia by
Berkeley Books, and in the United Kingdom and
Europe by Airlift Book Company.

Design by Nancy Austin
Food styling by Dan Becker
Prop styling by Carol Hacker

Library of Congress Cataloging-in-Publication Data

Hensperger, Beth.
Bread for breakfast / by Beth Hensperger
        p. cm.
    ISBN 1-58008-213-0
1. Bread. 2. Breakfasts. I. Title.
    TX769.H436 2000
641.8'15-dc21          00-056790

First printing 2001
Printed in Hong Kong

2  3  4  5  6  7  8  9  10 - 05  04  03  02

A cookbook project does not magically emerge completed, like the Roman kitchen-garden goddess, Venus, rising out of the sea, but only after long hours of forethought, labor, and collaboration. I can't imagine a nicer family than Ten Speed Press, who makes the process a pleasure: Lorena Jones, Aaron Wehner, and Nancy Austin. Thank you all.

Martha Casselman is the most fabulous agent anyone could ever have. I can't thank her enough for not only guiding me through the publishing world maze, but also for encouraging me to write with integrity and intuition. She has become my friend and confidante in the process.

For their input into this book, as well as my life, my heartfelt thanks to Marcie Ralston-Ansel, cornmeal-lovin' Judith Armenta, Jesse Cool, Nancy Cutler, Margaret Kuhl, Jacquie McMahan, Connie Rothermel, Nancyjo Terres, and Bobbe Torgerson, my trustworthy tester and sounding board. I also wish to thank food writers Marcy Goldman and Rose Beranbaum, who inspire me with their work.

And thanks to baker of cakes Patrick Coston for his friendship and interest.

# Contents

## Everyday Breakfast: Morning Toast and Jam......23

## Sunday Breakfast: Pancakes and Waffles......53

## Sweet Rolls: The Perfect Morning Fare......69

## Ethnic and Holiday Special Breads......99

## Entertaining for Breakfast: All Types of Coffee Cakes......119

## Butters, Jams, and Fruit and Cheese Spreads......141

# Introduction: Morning Fare Means More than Just a Buttered Slice

As cultures and tastes have evolved over the ages and across the continents, breakfast foods have retained much of their elemental quality, with breads playing a central role. Pictographs show ancient Egyptians eating a bread topped with poppyseeds, sesame seeds, and camphor, a cup of soured barley beer nearby. Their Assyrian contemporaries ate barley ash cakes, resembling flat stones, drizzled with date syrup. The early Romans served morning *jentaculum,* a humble meal consisting of a sturdy piece of spelt bread dipped in wine or spread with soft cheese and honey, before exercise or a visit to the baths. The medieval English sustained themselves on large slices of coarse mixed-grain breads called *maslin,* or thick oat griddle cakes and ale. The peasants of Hungary ate the traditional farmer's breakfast of roasted bacon on mammoth hunks of country bread washed down with *barackpálinka,* their beloved potent apricot brandy.

A quick tour through the contemporary cuisines of the world reveals an unmistakable continuity between breakfast then and now. Though commercial brands have supplanted more substantial and healthful homemade breads on many kitchen tables, today's breakfast breads represent a communion of sorts with past culinary habits. Greeks serve whole wheat rusks, *paximadia,* drizzled with mountain honey and olive oil and accompanied by cups of thick Turkish coffee or an herbal infusion from freshly gathered wild herbs or mint leaves. Italians savor their cups of *espresso del mattino* with squares of a sugared focaccia, and Spanish-speaking peoples, their *pan dulce* and *caffe con leche.* Germans wash down their poppyseed-topped imperial rolls with coffee so rich it is known as "black soup." Colombians consume their national corn flour flatbread-roll, the *arepa,* in two to three bites, washed down with hot chocolate. Scandinavians top stacks of thin pancakes with lingonberry preserves.

My breakfasts in the French countryside, where I lived for a time, were distinctly individual affairs. Upon first arriving in a village hamlet just a few miles outside the city of Tarbes, in the French Pyrenees, I wondered, where are the croissants? The poetic brioche? To my disappointment, I learned that folks living outside the cities served those foods only on Sundays, as they were considered too rich for daily consumption. It seemed that the croissant, one of the reasons I had come to France in the first place, was city café and hotel bed-tray fare.

Fortunately, I developed quite a fondness for the rituals and rhythms of *le petit déjeuner.* Daybreak would find me alone at a kitchen table set with the previous night's baguette, a crock of sweet butter, and a pot of jam. After boiling water on the small corner stove, I'd dip my spoon into a round tin with an ornate Russian label containing black tea flavored with vanilla and scoop the leaves into an old porcelain teapot. After a few minutes, I'd strain the lightly brewed tea into an oversized ceramic bowl with a small hairline crack on the side. After filling it to the top with milk, I'd cradle the bowl carefully with both hands and savor every fortifying sip. (Years later, I was delighted to have breakfast at Cafe Fanny in Berkeley, California, where they serve hot morning beverages in similarly large bowls.) I'd toast the day-old baguette, cut horizontally down the center to make two long, flat pieces that had to be pushed into the toaster because they were a bit too thick. This toast tasted so good, I often couldn't help but consume the rest of the loaf.

Considering our multicultural heritage, it's no surprise that breakfast in America means many things to many people. From the relatively spartan toast and jam, to a soul-warming plate of sausage gravy served up with buttermilk biscuits, to an elegant basket of mixed-berry muffins served with a steaming pot of coffee, everyone has a favorite way to start the day. Whatever people's allegiances may be, however, most would agree that no breakfast is complete without bread making an appearance.

I fondly recall my grandmother serving me prune juice in a diminutive glass and whole wheat toast spread with creamed, spiced honey butter when I visited with her; or when I stayed home from school in bed with a cold, my mother setting a tray on my bed with orange juice and a black-eyed Susan, the cooked egg nestled in the torn-out center hole of a slice of bread with the grilled butter-soaked "eye" perched enticingly on the side. Years later the oversized English china breakfast cup and saucer I bought for myself in a Knightsbridge dinnerware seconds shop became an integral part of my morning breakfast tea. Since the saucer was so large, my toasted cinnamon-swirl egg bread, cut in half on the diagonal and liberally soaked with butter right up to the crustline, easily balanced on each side of the saucer while I read the newspaper.

Morning baking can be one of life's most pleasurable, rewarding projects. Simple preparations tend to win out over elaborate stagings, whether guests are expected or the place setting is for one. Muffins, scones, and other quick breads are excellent choices, since prepping and baking times are kept to a minimum, but a special occasion is the perfect opportunity to experiment with a more challenging bread, such as a yeasted bread or holiday coffee cake. Even when our busy schedules don't allow time for morning baking, leftover breads come to the rescue, a wedge of last night's corn bread drizzled with maple syrup or a bagel with cream cheese tiding us over until midday.

Breakfast breads appeal to many different moods and have a place in an array of settings. A wholesome raisin bread with the crusts cut off, spread with peanut butter and served with a glass of milk to your child, is comforting and homey. A bran muffin, paired with a morning cappuccino, provides sustenance on the run when eaten at your desk. An early morning stack of fresh berry pancakes and a fruit smoothie shared with your best friend at a bustling restaurant are delightful and restorative. A homemade iced cinnamon roll or a strawberry dumpling and are coffee a bit of heaven when part of the intimate weekend breakfast-in-bed ritual.

Brunches are proudly exhibited meals that require a bit more preparation than everyday breakfasts. They are often planned affairs, with gala menus set out on a lavishly arranged buffet as a demonstration of hospitality and friendship, or arranged for family celebrations, such as a fête in observance of a religious holiday or a wedding. They are talked over, enjoyably lingered around, commented upon by guests who appreciate their host's efforts.

For brunches, I often serve a sweet bread basket on the buffet with a combination of oversized blueberry muffins, slices of poppyseed rolls, slices of a zucchini quick bread and a vanilla corn bread, chocolate chip scones, and jam-filled croissants. Such an assortment balances fruits, cheeses, chocolate, and nuts in a variety of shapes and sizes. Many of the more intricate traditional celebration breads often find their way onto the menu. The focus can be on a free-standing showpiece loaf, such as a fluted old-fashioned sour cream coffee cake on a pedestal plate or a flat coffee cake decorated with alternating rows of beautifully cut fruit, as in the rich fresh fruit kuchen, which is cut into squares and served right out of a handsome pan. All of my special-occasion breads are designed to feed many while adding flair to the table spread. My goal is to dazzle the eye as well as the palate.

I remember visiting a bustling restaurant for brunch after a long Sunday drive. The deceptively humble breadbasket was filled with an array of quick loaves in place of the usual sliced bread or crusty rolls. There were squares of an orange-flecked corn bread that sent me home to immediately bake a batch; a deliciously moist zucchini-pineapple bread; and a bright, tart fresh fruit muffin. We begged for refills.

Once I was invited to a traditional Russian brunch where they served only one sweet bread—the towering, mushroom-shaped *kulich*. The kulich, which is similar in taste, texture, and ingredients to the Italian *panettone,* was flanked by an impressive molded pyramid of fresh cheese, *pashka,* that served as the dramatic focal point. The delicate, yet substantial, yeast bread was over fourteen inches in height with a domed top dusted with powdered sugar, resembling freshly fallen snow. It was sliced in long, thin wedges and was spread with the soft, sugary cheese. This spectacular bread was to be eaten out of hand much in the same way as a long wedge of watermelon. I sat and stared at the bread, dazed by its dramatcially oversized proportions. Unwittingly, I had accepted an invitation to join a brotherhood of knowledgeable, artistic-epicurean eaters and fine bakers, and was expanding my appreciation of bread's many wonders.

In writing this book, I wanted to create a collection of the best breads for breakfast, including plain loaves for toast, as well as some quick-batter breads. I consider myself a traditional bread maker, paying respect to Old World sensibilities by using simple, yet high-quality, ingredients. I present recipes for familiar breakfast-table baked goods since they are likely to be made over and over, but there are also some newer breads you might not be familiar with. If you love sweets for breakfast, there is an array of pastries, coffee cakes, and muffins to satisfy, even if you are an "eat-as-you-go" sort of person. Make my favorite pancakes, waffles, muffins, and scones for Sunday morning, when there is a bit more time to fuss and linger. Here are some of the most beloved and beautiful, new- and old-fashioned breads and jams, swirled sweet rolls, fluffy egg breads and buns, fruit dumplings, nut and fruit breakfast breads, and fruit-topped coffee cakes, from my files to your table.

## Notes from My Kitchen

I put a lot of time, thought, and energy into my baking. I put an equal amount of the same into purchasing and obtaining quality ingredients and equipment. This care is just as basic to me as using the proper method in constructing a recipe. In other words, you can have all the technique in the world, but you won't get baked

goods that taste fantastic if you don't care about the ingredients that are essential to their makeup. Proper tools and equipment are secondary to good ingredients (I have tasted some great breads and muffins made under the most incredible circumstances with makeshift equipment), but certainly make the job more efficient and more satisfying. A nicely outfitted bakery kitchen is a source of pride, will last a lifetime, and will be a superb legacy to someone in your family who shares your interests.

# A Few Thoughts about How to Read a Recipe

How you interpret a recipe depends on your level of experience, it's as simple as that. While baking is often regarded as an elementary culinary skill, to be a great baker requires forethought in coordinating the components of preparation, as well as presentation. Unless you have made a recipe many times, the first step is to read through the recipe from start to finish. When I decide on a recipe, I begin by quickly reviewing the entire recipe, visualizing how the finished baked good will look and judging its appropriateness to the occasion. I ask, is it just for me, with all the extra going into the freezer? Is it geared to a child's palate (as every mother knows, nothing too weird or too messy)? Is it a gift and are these ingredients the receiving party likes? Is it for a party and will it adequately feed all the guests and be easy to serve?

In the second read-through I become more critical. I slow down, checking the ingredients list line by line and noting which ingredients I have on hand and what I need to buy. It never ceases to amaze me what I can miss on the first quick assessment. If the recipe is complicated, what can be made ahead and perhaps stored until the next day or frozen until needed? I look at the equipment called for. Do I have the right pan and electric mixer? Am I familiar with the techniques required? I check the baking time and make sure I have allotted enough time to assemble the ingredients, prepare the recipe, and be around the kitchen while the bread is in the oven.

Most of the recipes in this book are relatively simple, with the mixing of batters and doughs done in one bowl and little advance preparation required. My recipe headnotes include important information that will help you envision the final bread and then steer you through the process of making it. The instructions are written in a straightforward, easy to interpret manner, with essential information kept paramount. My goal is to guide you through the process of assembling, mixing, and baking your creation as quickly and smoothly as possible, so that the pure joy of your first bite is just around the corner. I hope you find all the breads as delicious to eat as they are beautiful to behold.

# Made from Scratch: Muffins, Loaves, Scones, and Corn Breads

A slice of pure Americana, quick breads in a variety of subtle flavors, muted colors, and dense textures are an integral part of my breakfast baking. Whether it's serving a mixed platter of moist, thick loaf slices, turning out muffins from a hot tin fresh from the oven, dropping hot biscuits into a waiting basket, or serving scones for a casual, late-breakfast tea, quick breads are an old-fashioned delight. The best thing about quick breads, besides eating them, is that they go from conception to completion in about an hour or less, cleanup included.

It's a ritual of sorts, gathering my favorite ingredients to bake my stash of quick breads—tart fresh cranberries; colorful dried apricots, sweet prunes, and amber dates; an array of nuts in appealing hues of brown; or musty-sweet stone-ground cornmeal. With my favorite recipes as a guide, I have mixed a batter or dough within fifteen minutes, made richer in flavor by the careful addition of sweet spices and liqueurs. During baking, the kitchen fills with a warm perfume. Once on the table, these breads always live up to their homey, down-to-earth reputation, never failing to please even the most discerning palate among my friends and relatives.

*Early Morning Fruit Muffins (page 4) and*
*Lemon and Blueberry Bread with Lemon Glaze (page 14)*

# Tips for Baking Perfect Muffins, Loaves, Scones, and Biscuits

- I usually mix quick-bread batters by hand, since only a few strokes are needed to blend the ingredients. The best tool I have found for this is a sturdy, long-handled Danish dough whisk, which looks like a cross between a spoon and a spatula (available from King Arthur Baker's Catalog), or a medium balloon whisk.

- Disposable and reusable foil pans, available in a variety of sizes at the supermarket, are excellent for baking quick loaves.

- Quick breads require an accurate oven temperature for proper baking. If you suspect your oven temperature is not accurate, invest in an oven thermometer.

- If you are using a glass, Pyrex, or dark-finish baking pan, lower the oven temperature required in the recipe by 25° to prevent overbaking.

- Invest in a metal cake tester—a rigid stainless steel wire with a loop handle. This is the best tool for inserting into the center of a quick bread or muffin to judge if it is finished baking.

- To set the crumb, allow quick loaves to cool completely before slicing. Use a serrated knife to cut quick loaves; this preserves the delicate crumb. Many recipes recommend letting the loaf rest overnight or refrigerating the loaf to improve flavor. Biscuits and scones are best right out of the oven, and muffins are good warm or reheated.

# Supernatural Bran Muffins with Dates

*Bran is the outer layer of the wheat kernel, and the germ is its inner embryo. Bran is high in calcium, phosphorus, and complex carbohydrates, while the germ has a cache of minerals, vitamins, and protein. These bran muffins are some of the best I have ever come across, and so tasty you won't suspect how good they are for you. They are a snap to mix, and the resulting batter is beautifully fluffy and an earthy brown from the generous amount of fiber-rich bran and wheat germ. The fragrance of orange wafts up from the just-baked muffins.*

1. Preheat the oven to 375°. Grease the cups of a standard 2¾-inch muffin tin.

2. In a medium bowl, combine the all-purpose and whole wheat flours, bran, sugar, wheat germ, baking soda, cinnamon, baking powder, and salt.

3. In another medium bowl, combine the eggs, oil, buttermilk, and orange juice concentrate with a large spoon or dough whisk. Add the wet to the dry ingredients, stirring until just moistened. Fold in the dates using a large rubber spatula just until evenly distributed, no more than a few strokes. The batter will be delightfully fluffy.

4. Spoon the batter into the muffin tin, filling each prepared cup full to the rim. Bake on the center rack of the oven for 20 to 24 minutes, or until golden and the tops are dry and springy to the touch and a cake tester inserted into the center of a muffin comes out clean. Remove the pan from the oven and serve the muffins warm with butter. The muffins can be stored in the freezer in plastic freezer bags for up to 3 months.

*Makes 12 muffins*

2 cups unbleached all-purpose flour

½ cup whole wheat pastry flour

1 cup raw wheat bran

⅓ cup firmly packed light brown sugar

¼ cup toasted wheat germ

2½ teaspoons baking soda

1 teaspoon ground cinnamon

½ teaspoon baking powder

½ teaspoon salt

2 large eggs

½ cup vegetable or canola oil

1½ cups cultured buttermilk

½ cup orange juice concentrate, thawed and undiluted

6 ounces pitted dates, chopped (about 1¼ cups), or 2 cups fresh or frozen blueberries

# Every Morning Fruit Muffins (Illustrated on page xviii)

**Makes 9 muffins**

1½ cups unbleached all-purpose
flour

¼ cup whole wheat or graham flour

¼ cup firmly packed light or
dark brown sugar

2 teaspoons baking powder

½ teaspoon baking soda

½ teaspoon salt

2 large eggs

¼ cup vegetable oil, light olive oil,
or nut oil

¾ cup cultured buttermilk

2 tablespoons sour cream or
plain yogurt

1 teaspoon pure vanilla extract

2½ cups chopped fresh fruit
(see suggestions)

*I started making these fruit-laden muffins when friends would show up unexpectedly on a weekend morning. I know the recipe by heart and can chat casually while looking around the kitchen for whatever fresh fruit is on the counter. Guests hardly notice me whipping the batter together and are always surprised when the muffins are on the table in about an hour.*

1.  Preheat the oven to 375°. Grease 9 cups of a standard 2¾-inch muffin tin.

2.  In a medium bowl, combine the all-purpose and whole wheat flours, sugar, baking powder, baking soda, and salt.

3.  In another medium bowl, combine the eggs, oil, buttermilk, sour cream or yogurt, and vanilla with a large spoon or dough whisk. Add to the dry ingredients, stirring until just moistened. Add the fruit to the batter, and fold in using a large rubber spatula just until the fruit is evenly distributed, no more than a few strokes, taking care not to break up the fruit.

4.  Spoon the batter into the muffin tin, filling each prepared cup full to the rim. Fill the empty muffin cups halfway with water to prevent the pan from buckling. Bake on the center rack of the oven for 20 to 25 minutes, or until golden and the tops are dry and springy to the touch and a cake tester inserted into the center of a muffin comes out clean. Remove the pan from the oven and serve the muffins warm with butter. The muffins can be stored in the freezer in plastic freezer bags for up to 3 months.

## Peach Muffins

Add 2½ cups peeled, stoned, and chopped fresh peaches or drained, canned unsweetened peaches. I also like to add ½ teaspoon ground mace or nutmeg with the dry ingredients.

## Pear Muffins

Add 2½ cups peeled, cored, and chopped fresh firm pears. I also like to add 1 teaspoon ground cinnamon or cardamom with the dry ingredients.

## Plum Muffins

Add 2½ cups peeled, stoned, and chopped fresh plums. I also like to add ½ teaspoon ground cinnamon with the dry ingredients.

## Raspberry Muffins

Add 2½ cups fresh raspberries and increase the sugar to ½ cup in the dry ingredients.

# Walnut Rye Muffins

Makes 9 muffins

²⁄₃ cup chopped walnuts

1¾ cups whole wheat pastry flour

¼ cup light or medium rye flour

1 tablespoon firmly packed light or
    dark brown sugar

2½ teaspoons baking powder

½ teaspoon baking soda

¾ teaspoon salt

1 cup cultured buttermilk

½ cup small curd cottage cheese

2 large eggs

3 tablespoons unsalted butter or
    margarine, melted

9 walnut halves, optional

*Walnuts contain polyunsaturated fat, the same type of "good" fat found in pumpkin and sunflower seeds, making it a healthy nut to eat on a regular basis. Matched with a bit of rye flour, walnuts form one of the most classic food pairings in the culinary world. These are some of my favorite muffins; they taste wonderfully rich and are just as good served with cheese for lunch as they are served with jam for breakfast.*

1. Preheat the oven to 375°. Grease 9 cups of a standard 2¾-inch muffin tin.

2. Spread the walnuts on an ungreased baking sheet and place in the center of the oven for 4 to 5 minutes to lightly toast. Set aside to cool.

3. In a large bowl, combine the whole wheat and rye flours, sugar, baking powder, baking soda, salt, and toasted nuts. In a medium bowl, beat the buttermilk, cottage cheese, eggs, and melted butter with a whisk just to blend. Pour the buttermilk mixture into the flour mixture and stir with a large rubber spatula just until moistened, no more than 15 to 20 strokes.

4. Spoon the batter into the muffin tin, filling each prepared cup three-quarters full. Place a walnut half on top of the batter in each cup. Fill the empty muffin cups halfway with water to prevent the pan from buckling. Bake on the center rack of the oven for 20 to 25 minutes, or until browned around the edges and sides and the tops are dry to the touch. A cake tester inserted into the center should come out clean. Remove the pan from the oven and remove the muffins to cool slightly on a rack, or pile them in a basket. Serve warm with butter. The muffins can be stored in the freezer in plastic freezer bags for up to 3 months.

# Sweet Cornmeal Pecan Muffins

*This recipe came from an old friend's mother who grew up in the South. It surprised me when I first made it, since the batter is remarkably thin but bakes up into a tender, rich muffin. At once earthy and sweet, these muffins have a wonderful flavor and moist texture.*

1. Preheat the oven to 400°. Grease the cups of a standard 2¾-inch muffin tin.

2. In a medium bowl, combine the cornmeal, pecans, flour, sugar, baking powder, and salt.

3. In another medium bowl, combine the eggs, melted butter, vanilla, and milk with a whisk. Add to the dry ingredients, stirring until just moistened with a large rubber spatula or dough whisk. The batter will be thin.

4. Spoon the batter into the muffin tin, filling each prepared cup three-quarters full (the muffin will rise and make a high dome). Bake on the center rack of the oven for 18 to 23 minutes, or until lightly golden brown and the tops are dry and springy to the touch and a cake tester inserted into the center of a muffin comes out clean. Remove the pan from the oven and cool in the pan for 5 minutes before removing the muffins to cool slightly on a rack. Serve warm. The muffins can be stored in the freezer in plastic freezer bags for up to 3 months.

*Makes 12 muffins*

1¼ cups yellow cornmeal, preferably stone-ground

1 cup chopped pecans

¾ cup unbleached all-purpose flour

1 cup sugar

2 teaspoons baking powder

½ teaspoon salt

2 large eggs

8 tablespoons (1 stick) unsalted butter, melted

1 teaspoon pure vanilla extract

1 cup milk

# Sugar-Free Banana Pecan Muffins

Makes 9 muffins

2 cups whole wheat pastry flour

1 ½ teaspoons baking powder

1 teaspoon ground cinnamon

½ teaspoon baking soda

½ teaspoon salt

½ cup chopped pecans

1 cup cultured buttermilk

2 large eggs

½ cup pecan oil or canola oil,
    or a blend of the two

2 ripe bananas, mashed (about
    1 ¼ cups)

1 teaspoon pure vanilla extract

*It all started simply enough—I wanted to make a muffin with no added sugar. I found that crushed fruit and fruit juices provided enough natural sugar that I didn't miss the added sugar at all. What I ended up with is my favorite banana muffin.*

1. Preheat the oven to 375°. Grease 9 cups of a standard 2¾-inch muffin tin.

2. In a large bowl, combine the flour, cinnamon, baking powder, baking soda, salt, and pecans.

3. In a medium bowl, beat the buttermilk, eggs, and oil with a dough whisk for 1 minute. Add the banana and vanilla. Pour into the flour mixture and stir using a large rubber spatula just until moistened, no more than 15 to 20 strokes. The batter will be lumpy.

4. Immediately spoon the batter into the muffin tin, filling each prepared cup full to the rim. Fill the empty muffin cups halfway with water to prevent the pan from buckling. Bake on the center rack of the oven until browned, the tops feel dry and springy, and a cake tester inserted into the center of a muffin comes out clean, 20 to 25 minutes. Do not overbake or the muffins will be too dry. Remove the pan from the oven and let the muffins rest in the pan for 5 minutes before turning them out onto a rack to cool. The muffins can be stored in the freezer in plastic freezer bags for up to 3 months.

# Sugar-Free Orange Blueberry Muffins

*What would breakfast be without the requisite blueberry muffin, fresh from the oven? These muffins are made with fresh orange or tangerine juice; frozen juices tend to be a bit bitter.*

1. Preheat the oven to 375°. Grease 10 cups of a standard 2¾-inch muffin tin.

2. In a large bowl, combine the flour, baking powder, cinnamon, nutmeg, and salt.

3. In a measuring cup, combine the oil and orange juice. Make a well in the center of the dry mixture and add the eggs and juice mixture. Beat with a dough whisk for 1 minute, just until moistened, no more than 15 to 20 strokes. Using a large rubber spatula, fold in the blueberries.

4. Immediately spoon the batter into the muffin tin, filling each prepared cup to the rim. Fill the empty muffin cups halfway with water to prevent the pan from buckling. Bake on the center rack of the oven until browned, the tops feel dry and springy, and a cake tester inserted into the center of a muffin comes out clean, 20 to 25 minutes. Do not overbake, or muffins will be too dry. Remove the pan from the oven and let the muffins rest in the pan for 5 minutes before turning them out onto a rack to cool to room temperature. The muffins can be stored in the freezer in plastic freezer bags for up to 3 months.

1¾ cups unbleached all-purpose flour

1 tablespoon baking powder

1½ teaspoons ground cinnamon

½ teaspoon ground nutmeg

½ teaspoon salt

¼ cup walnut oil

¾ cup fresh orange or tangerine juice

3 large eggs

2 cups fresh blueberries, rinsed, picked over, and drained on a kitchen towel, or frozen, unthawed blueberries

# Biscuit Muffins

Makes 12 muffins

2½ cups unbleached all-purpose flour

¼ cup sugar

1 tablespoon plus ½ teaspoon baking powder

¼ teaspoon baking soda

1 teaspoon ground cardamom or nutmeg

1 teaspoon salt

10 tablespoons (1 stick plus 2 table-spoons) cold unsalted butter, cut into small pieces

1 cup cold cultured buttermilk

1 tablespoon sugar, for sprinkling, optional

*A friend had these crusty muffins in the breadbasket at K-Paul's restaurant in New Orleans and brought the recipe back to me. The recipe is mixed like a biscuit batter, but then baked in a muffin tin, which is tremendously convenient. The muffins are such delightfully simple morning fare that you will make them as much as my circle of friends does (the recipe has circulated faster than e-mail). The recipe also makes a great shortcake as well as an eat-out-of-hand muffin, ever so satisfying served warm from the oven with butter and jam.*

1. Preheat the oven to 350°. Grease the cups of a standard 2¾-inch muffin tin.

2. In a large bowl or in the workbowl of a heavy-duty electric mixer fitted with the paddle attachment, combine the flour, sugar, baking powder, baking soda, cardamom, and salt. Distribute the butter over the top of the flour mixture. Using a fork or with the electric mixer on low speed, cut in the butter for 2 to 3 minutes, until the mixture resembles coarse crumbs laced with small chunks of butter.

3. Turn off the mixer, if using, and pour the buttermilk into the center of the dough. Using a fork or with the mixer on low speed, mix until the dough forms a sticky mass, about 30 seconds. Increase the speed to medium for about 10 seconds; the mass will form a moist, sticky clump on the paddle and clear the sides of the bowl. Do not overmix; you are just lightly mixing the dough and letting it pull together.

4. Lightly dust a work surface with flour. Scrape the dough off the fork or paddle with a rubber spatula or plastic dough card. Scrape the sides and bottom of the bowl and add the batter to the mass of dough. Sprinkle the top with some flour. With floured fingers, fold the dough over and gently knead for 6 to 8 gentle strokes, leaving the dough very soft and as sticky as possible. Using a dough card, cut the dough into 12 equal portions; they will be lumpy and uneven. Place each dough piece in a muffin cup, sprinkle with some sugar, and press lightly to fill the cups.

5. Bake on the center rack of the oven for 25 to 30 minutes, or until firm to the touch and the tops and bottoms are golden brown. Remove the pan from the oven and transfer the muffins to the cooling rack to cool for a few minutes before serving.

# Pineapple Zucchini Bread

Makes two 9 by 5-inch loaves

3 cups unbleached all-purpose flour

1 cup chopped walnuts or pecans

2 teaspoons baking soda

½ teaspoon baking powder

1½ teaspoons ground cinnamon

1 teaspoon ground allspice

1 teaspoon salt

3 large eggs

¾ cup vegetable oil

1 cup firmly packed light brown sugar

1 cup granulated sugar

2 teaspoons pure vanilla extract

2½ cups shredded zucchini

1 (8½-ounce) can crushed, unsweetened pineapple in its own juice, drained

*Zucchini makes a superior quick bread, moist and green flecked. The cylindrical shape of the summer vegetable is easy to hold in your hand and grate (I use the large holes on my handheld grater since the smaller holes leave you with a pile of mush). Zucchini has a high water content, so no added liquid is needed in making this bread. This particular zucchini bread is light and takes well to spices, nuts, and fruits, my favorite being pineapple. Pyrex loaf pans let me see how brown the bottom crust is, but I must admit I love disposable aluminum pans, of which I always have a stack (you can wash them in the dishwasher on the top rack and reuse them until they are misshapen). Once out of the oven, this bread begs to be eaten warm in thick slices.*

1.  Place the oven rack in the lower third position and preheat the oven to 350° (325° if using Pyrex or dark-finish loaf pans). Grease two 9 by 5-inch loaf pans.

2.  In a medium bowl, combine the flour, nuts, baking soda, baking powder, cinnamon, allspice, and salt.

3.  In a large bowl or in the workbowl of a heavy-duty electric mixer fitted with the paddle attachment, combine the eggs, oil, sugars, and vanilla. Using a whisk or with the electric mixer on medium speed, beat the ingredients until thick and fluffy, about 2 minutes. Fold in the zucchini and pineapple using a large rubber spatula or dough whisk. Add the flour mixture in 3 additions with the spatula, stirring lightly between each addition. Stir well to make a just-moistened batter that is evenly combined (there should be no patches of flour), about 25 strokes; do not overmix.

4. Divide the batter evenly between the prepared pans. Bake on the rack for 55 to 60 minutes, or until the edges pull away slightly from the sides of the pan and a cake tester inserted into the center comes out clean. Let the loaves rest in the pan for 5 minutes before turning out onto a rack to cool, right side up. Serve in thick slices, or store at room temperature, wrapped tightly in plastic wrap, for up to 3 days.

# Lemon and Blueberry Bread
## with Lemon Glaze (Illustrated on page xviii)

*Makes one 9 by 5-inch loaf*

1 ½ cups unbleached all-purpose
flour

1 teaspoon baking soda

½ teaspoon baking powder

Grated zest of 2 lemons

¼ teaspoon salt

6 tablespoons (¾ stick) unsalted
butter, at room temperature

1 cup sugar

2 large eggs

⅔ cup cultured buttermilk

1 ¾ cups fresh blueberries, picked
over, rinsed, and drained on a
kitchen towel, or 1 (12-ounce)
package unsweetened, unthawed
frozen blueberries

2 tablespoons finely chopped
candied ginger or candied
lemon peel

LEMON GLAZE

¼ cup sugar

3 tablespoons freshly squeezed
lemon juice

*Here is a wonderful lemon bread recipe inspired by the ever prolific lemon tree outside my kitchen door. Blueberries and lemon are a dramatic and popular flavor duo all year round. (See Lemon Yogurt Pancakes, page 58, for another luscious lemon delight.) You can find the candied ginger in the spice section of the supermarket or in specialty food stores.*

1. Preheat the oven to 325° (300° if using a Pyrex or dark-finish pan). Grease a 9 by 5-inch loaf pan.

2. Combine the flour, baking soda, baking powder, lemon zest, and salt in a small bowl.

3. In a large bowl using a whisk or in a heavy-duty electric mixer fitted with the paddle attachment on low speed, cream the butter and sugar until light and fluffy, about 1 minute. Add the eggs, one at a time, beating well after each addition. Add the dry ingredients to the creamed mixture in 2 equal portions, alternating with the buttermilk in 2 additions. Beat just until smooth, about 1 minute. With a large rubber spatula, carefully fold in the blueberries (you do not want to break up or mash the berries) and candied ginger or lemon peel.

4. Using a rubber spatula, scrape the batter into the prepared loaf pan. Bake on the center rack of the oven for 65 to 75 minutes, or until golden brown, especially around the edges, and a cake tester inserted into the center of the loaf comes out clean. Remove from the oven and place on a cooling rack.

5. Meanwhile, to make the lemon glaze, combine the sugar and lemon juice in a small saucepan or microwave-safe bowl. Place over low heat or in the microwave oven until the sugar just dissolves.

6. Pierce the hot loaf several times straight through from the top to the bottom with a wooden skewer. Immediately pour the hot lemon syrup over the bread; it will soak in. Cool for 30 minutes in the pan before turning out onto a rack to cool completely. As the bread cools, the syrup will dry into a glaze. Let the bread stand at room temperature until ready to serve, or wrap tightly in plastic wrap and store in the refrigerator for up to 4 days.

# Oatmeal Applesauce Bread

Makes one 9 by 5-inch loaf

1 ¼ cups unbleached all-purpose flour

1 cup quick-cooking rolled oats

⅔ cup firmly packed light brown sugar

½ cup chopped dried apples

1 ½ teaspoons ground cinnamon or apple pie spice mixture

½ teaspoon ground nutmeg

1 ½ teaspoons baking powder

1 teaspoon baking soda

1 teaspoon salt

1 ¼ cups unsweetened applesauce

⅓ cup vegetable oil or canola oil

2 large eggs

⅓ cup cultured buttermilk

**SPICED PECAN CRUMBS**

¼ cup pecans

2 tablespoons firmly packed light brown sugar

2 tablespoons firmly packed dark brown sugar

½ teaspoon ground cinnamon or apple pie spice

*Applesauce can be a prominent flavor in a batter or, as in this recipe, a secret ingredient for adding flavor, moisture, and great texture to a quick bread. I like to layer this bread with finely ground pecans and brown sugar, the same mixture I use for the layering effect in coffee cakes. I usually make a double batch of the crumb topping and keep the extra in the freezer, ready to sprinkle on top of breads or muffins, so I can cut down on my work time when baking for breakfast. Apple pie spice is a commercial blend of cinnamon, nutmeg, mace, and cloves.*

1. Preheat the oven to 350° (325° if using a Pyrex or dark-finish pan). Grease a 9 by 5-inch loaf pan.

2. In a mixing bowl, combine the flour, rolled oats, brown sugar, dried apples, cinnamon, nutmeg, baking powder, baking soda, and salt. Set aside.

3. To make the spiced pecan crumbs, place the pecans, light and dark brown sugars, and cinnamon in the workbowl of a food processor. Pulse to finely chop the nuts. The mixture will have a sandy texture. Set aside.

4. Combine the applesauce, oil, eggs, and buttermilk in a small bowl and beat with a whisk until smooth. Make a well in the center of the dry ingredients and stir in the applesauce mixture with a large rubber spatula or dough whisk. The batter will be slightly lumpy. Do not overmix.

5. Using a large rubber spatula, scrape half of the batter into the prepared loaf pan (I like the surface of the batter to be uneven so there is a gentle swirl effect inside after baking). Sprinkle

with half of the spiced pecan crumbs, top with the rest of the batter, and sprinkle the remaining crumbs over the top.

6. Bake on the center rack of the oven for 55 to 65 minutes, or until the top is firm to the touch, the loaf pulls away from the sides of the pan, and a cake tester inserted into the center comes out clean. Remove from the oven and place on a cooling rack to rest for 15 minutes before turning out of the pan and cooling to room temperature. Do not slice before the loaf cools completely or it will clump.

# Old-Fashioned Oatmeal Scones

*Oatmeal scones are as special as they are simple. Popular in Wales, Scotland, and Ireland, they are enjoyed for breakfast—believe it or not—with a pint of ale (cream cheese and smoked salmon are more to my taste). Here the scones are made with buttermilk, which creates a creamy colored, moist little bread. I use McCann's oatmeal, imported from Ireland and available in well-stocked supermarkets; it has a wonderful, full flavor. You can also serve these, split, as a rustic shortcake.*

**Makes 12 scones**

- 1 cup unbleached all-purpose flour
- ¾ cup whole wheat pastry flour
- ⅓ cup firmly packed light brown sugar or raw sugar
- 2 teaspoons baking powder
- ¾ teaspoon baking soda
- ½ teaspoon salt
- 12 tablespoons (1½ sticks) cold unsalted butter, cut into small pieces
- 1¼ cups quick-cooking rolled oats
- ½ cup currants
- 1 cup cold buttermilk, plus more, as needed

1. Preheat the oven to 375°. Line a baking sheet with parchment.

2. In a large bowl or in the workbowl of a heavy-duty electric mixer fitted with the paddle attachment, combine the all-purpose and whole wheat flours, sugar, baking powder, baking soda, and salt. Using a fork or with the electric mixer on low speed, cut in the butter until it has the texture of soft crumbs. Add the oatmeal and currants, and toss to combine.

3. Stir in the buttermilk until the dough forms in a soft, shaggy ball, adding more buttermilk 1 tablespoon at a time, as needed.

4. Turn the dough out onto a lightly floured work surface and knead gently about 10 times, or just until the dough holds together. Roll or pat out the dough into a rectangle 1 inch thick, 9 inches wide, and 12 inches long. Cut with a sharp knife or pastry wheel to form 12 squares (3 cuts across and 4 cuts down).

5. Place the pieces ½ inch apart on the parchment-lined baking sheet. Bake on the center rack of the oven for 15 to 20 minutes, or until golden brown. Remove the pan from the oven and cool to the desired temperature on the baking sheet. Serve hot, warm, or at room temperature.

# Apricot, White Chocolate, and Walnut Scones

*The first time I came across this combination of ingredients, I thought it unusual and probably too sweet. Luckily I went ahead and made these scones, and I am now a committed fan of the sumptuous trio of white chocolate, dried fruit, and nuts. These scones are perfect for a fancier breakfast or brunch, and they make a special gift for a loved one.*

1.  Preheat the oven to 375°. Line a baking sheet with parchment.

2.  In a large bowl or in the workbowl of a heavy-duty electric mixer fitted with the paddle attachment, combine the flour, sugar, baking powder, baking soda, and salt. Using a fork or with the electric mixer on low speed, cut in the butter until it has the texture of soft crumbs.

3.  In a medium bowl, whisk together the eggs, vanilla, and buttermilk. Pour this mixture into the flour mixture and stir until the dough forms a soft, shaggy ball, adding additional buttermilk 1 tablespoon at a time, as needed. Add the white chocolate, walnuts, and apricots, stirring until evenly distributed.

4.  Turn the dough out onto a lightly floured work surface and knead gently about 10 times, or just until the dough holds together. Divide the dough into 2 equal portions. Pat each dough piece into a 1-inch-thick round, 6 inches in diameter. Using a sharp knife, cut each round into 4 wedges.

5.  Place the wedges ½ inch apart on the baking sheet. Bake on the center rack of the oven 15 to 20 minutes, or until golden brown. Remove the pan from the oven and cool on the baking sheet. Serve the scones at room temperature the day they are baked.

*Makes 8 scones*

2 cups unbleached all-purpose flour

2 tablespoons sugar

2 teaspoons baking powder

¼ teaspoon baking soda

½ teaspoon salt

4 tablespoons (½ stick) cold unsalted butter, cut into small pieces

2 large eggs

1½ teaspoons pure vanilla extract

½ cup cold buttermilk, plus more, as needed

4 ounces white chocolate, cut into ½-inch chunks, or ¾ cup white chocolate chips

¾ cup coarsely chopped walnuts

¾ cup chopped dried apricots

# The Kids' Corn Bread

*Makes one 8-inch round bread*

¾ cup unbleached all-purpose flour

⅔ cup yellow cornmeal, preferably
  stone-ground

1 tablespoon toasted wheat germ

1 tablespoon baking powder

1 teaspoon salt

1 large egg

1 cup cultured buttermilk

3 tablespoons unsalted butter,
  melted

2 tablespoons honey

3 tablespoons orange marmalade

*This simple corn bread is so good that the little ones will never guess at the extra ingredients of wheat germ and marmalade. The addition of orange marmalade to the batter is a memorable one, and you will be searching for the precious bits of it in each wedge. This is a very moist bread, so I let it stand until it is room temperature or make it the night before and reheat. Serve it with butter or margarine.*

1. Preheat the oven to 400° (375° if using a Pyrex or dark-finish pan). Grease an 8-inch round metal or Pyrex pan or a ceramic souffle dish.

2. Combine the flour, cornmeal, wheat germ, baking powder, and salt in a large bowl.

3. Make a well in the center of the dry ingredients and add the egg, buttermilk, butter, honey, and marmalade. Using a large spoon or dough whisk, stir just until all of the ingredients are moistened yet thoroughly blended; take care not to overmix.

4. Pour the batter into the prepared pan and bake on the center rack of the oven for about 20 to 25 minutes, or until dark golden around the edges and a cake tester inserted into the center comes out clean. The top should feel firm to the touch. Let stand for 30 minutes in the pan before cutting into thick wedges.

# Vanilla Breakfast Corn Bread

*This sweet, moist corn bread has a delicate aroma and grainy texture from the cornmeal. During the summer berry season, try adding 1½ cups fresh blueberries or raspberries to the batter for variation. Serve this bread with sliced fresh papaya and sweet butter for an unusual, utterly divine breakfast meal.*

1. Preheat the oven to 350° (325° if using a Pyrex or dark-finish pan). Grease an 8-inch springform pan or 8-inch square Pyrex pan.

2. Combine the cornmeal, flour, sugar, salt, baking powder, and baking soda in a large bowl.

3. In a small bowl, mix the eggs, buttermilk, and vanilla with a wooden spoon or dough whisk until combined. Add to the dry ingredients and pour the melted butter over the top of the batter. Stir just until all of the ingredients are moistened yet thoroughly blended; take care not to overmix.

4. Pour the batter into the prepared pan and bake on the center rack of the oven for 40 to 45 minutes, or until golden around the edges and a cake tester inserted into the center comes out clean. Let stand for 15 minutes in the pan before cutting into thick wedges.

Makes one 8-inch round bread

1 cup yellow cornmeal, preferably stone-ground

1 cup unbleached all-purpose flour

¾ cup confectioners' sugar

½ teaspoon salt

½ teaspoon baking powder

½ teaspoon baking soda

2 large eggs

1¼ cups cultured buttermilk

1 tablespoon pure vanilla extract

6 tablespoons (¾ stick) unsalted butter, melted

# Everyday Breakfast: Morning Toast and Jam

**M**orning toast is an American institution, and a basic loaf of bread is all that is required to honor it. At once delicious, nourishing, filling, and satisfying, such loaves are easy enough for a fledgling baker to create and perfectly suited for everyday eating. A good loaf of bread features wholesome grains, dairy products, and eggs in a hearty array of combinations, and utilizes the time-honored techniques practiced by all yeast bakers. These are straightforward doughs, not fussy or complicated. Only the whole wheat bread has a short sponge, which is well worth the extra work since it contributes greatly to the texture of the finished loaf. This chapter is not about "whipping it up," however. Though most of these breads have a short, easy-to-assemble list of ingredients, you must plan your time and make them the day ahead of when you want to eat them. Rushing through their creation won't do, since much of their character develops during the crucial rising stage. Read each recipe carefully before you begin—that way, you will feel more composed than if you haphazardly try to pull together all of the elements during the work phase.

I've included my favorite toast breads—orange, buttermilk, oatmeal, cinnamon, and, of course, the ultimate raisin bread. You'll also find two rather unique recipes, for bagel bread and English muffin bread; these have a familiar character, flavor, and texture since the doughs are adapted from those used in the more time-consuming versions of these bakery staples.

*Oatmeal Egg Bread with a Cinnamon Swirl (page 32)*

# Buttermilk White Bread

Makes two 8 by 4½-inch loaves

1 cup warm water (105° to 115°)

1 tablespoon (1 package) active
  dry yeast

Pinch of light brown sugar

1¼ cups warm buttermilk
  (105° to 115°)

4 tablespoons (½ stick) unsalted
  butter or margarine, melted

3 tablespoons firmly packed
  light brown sugar

1 tablespoon salt

5½ to 6 cups unbleached
  all-purpose or bread flour

*Beginning bakers, rejoice! Here is a foolproof bread that will make fantastic toast. If you want to eat it warm from the oven, you can make the dough a day ahead and bake the loaves in the morning. As long as the bread cools for at least 30 minutes, it will be fine to slice warm. Everyone will swoon over this easy and delicious bread, which has a flavor and texture that is rarely available with store-bought bread.*

1. Place ⅓ cup of the warm water in a small bowl. Sprinkle the yeast and pinch of sugar over the water and stir to dissolve. Let the mixture stand until foamy, about 10 minutes.

2. Combine the remaining water, the buttermilk, butter, sugar, salt, and 2 cups of the flour in a large bowl or in the workbowl of a heavy-duty electric mixer fitted with the paddle attachment. Using a whisk or with the electric mixer on low speed, beat until smooth, about 1 minute. Add the yeast mixture and 1 cup of the flour and beat for 1 minute more. Add the remaining flour, ½ cup at a time, to form a soft dough that just clears the sides of the bowl (switch to a wooden spoon when necessary if making by hand).

3. Turn the dough out onto a lightly floured work surface and knead until smooth and springy, about 1 minute for a machine-mixed dough and 3 minutes for a hand-mixed dough. Add 1 tablespoon of flour at a time, as necessary, to prevent sticking. Place the dough in a greased deep container (such as a plastic bucket), turn once to coat the top, and cover loosely with plastic wrap. Let rise at room temperature until doubled in bulk, about 2 hours. If refrigerating the dough overnight, just cover the container with a double layer of plastic wrap and refrigerate.

4. Grease two 8 by 4½-inch loaf pans (clay pans are wonderful for this crusty bread). Turn out the dough onto the work surface and divide into 2 equal portions. Form the dough into 2 rectangular shapes and place in the prepared pans. Cover loosely with plastic wrap and let rise at room temperature until doubled in bulk, or until the dough is about an inch above the rims of the pans, 45 minutes to 1 hour (about 4 hours if the dough has been refrigerated).

5. Preheat the oven to 375° (350° if using a Pyrex or dark-finish pan) 20 minutes before baking. Place the oven rack in the lower third position of the oven.

6. Using a serrated knife, cut a long slash no deeper than ¼ inch down the length of the loaves. Bake for 40 to 45 minutes, or until the loaves are golden brown and the bottoms sound hollow when tapped with your finger. Immediately remove the loaves from the pans and transfer to racks to cool completely before slicing.

## Jam Toasts ❈ *Makes 16 toast fingers; serves 4 to 6*

*Here's a great way to finish a loaf of day-old bread. My favorites for these sandwiches are Buttermilk White Bread (page 24), Orange Bread (page 26), or Applesauce Bread (page 28). I use cooking spray to reduce the fat, but you can use butter or margarine if you prefer. Serve with tall glasses of milk and fresh fruit.*

8 (¼-inch) slices homemade bread, sliced from the center of the loaf

1 cup thick jam

Butter-flavored vegetable cooking spray

1. Spread 4 slices of bread almost to the edges with jam. Top with another slice of bread and press down. Spray each side of the sandwich with the vegetable cooking spray.

2. Heat a flat or ridged skillet over medium-high heat until hot. Cook the sandwiches until golden brown and crisp, 3 minutes on each side. Remove the sandwiches from the skillet with a metal spatula, place on a cutting board, and cut each into 4 strips. Serve immediately.

# Orange Bread

Makes 2 round loaves

¼ cup warm water (105° to 115°)

1 tablespoon (1 package) active
    dry yeast

Pinch of sugar

½ cup warm milk (105° to 115°)

1¼ cups freshly squeezed
    orange juice

2 teaspoons pure vanilla extract

½ cup sugar

4 tablespoons (½ stick) unsalted
    butter, melted

1 large egg

Grated zest of 1 orange

5½ to 6 cups bread flour

2 teaspoons salt

*This bread has a delicate orange flavor and a fabulous texture. It is as much a favorite with children as it is with adults, and it makes very special toast (pass the jam, please!). It also makes a delicious, tangy French toast.*

1.  Place the warm water in a small bowl. Sprinkle the yeast and pinch of sugar over the water and stir to dissolve. Let the mixture stand until foamy, about 10 minutes.

2.  Combine the milk, orange juice, vanilla, sugar, butter, egg, zest, and 1½ cups of the flour in a large bowl or in the workbowl of a heavy-duty electric mixer fitted with the paddle attachment. Using a whisk or with the electric mixer on low speed, beat until smooth, about 1 minute. Add the yeast mixture, salt, and 1 cup of the flour. Beat 1 minute more. Add the remaining flour, ½ cup at a time, to form a soft dough that just clears the sides of the bowl (switch to a wooden spoon when necessary if making by hand).

3.  Turn the dough out onto a lightly floured work surface and knead until smooth and springy, about 1 minute for a machine-mixed dough and 3 minutes for a hand-mixed dough. Add 1 tablespoon of flour at a time, as necessary, to prevent sticking. Place the dough in a greased deep container (such as a plastic bucket), turn once to coat the top, and cover loosely with plastic wrap. Let rise at room temperature until doubled in bulk, about 1½ hours.

4. Line a baking sheet with parchment paper. Turn the dough out onto the work surface, divide into 2 equal portions, and form each into a compact, round loaf. Place the loaves seam side down on the baking sheet, cover loosely with plastic wrap, and let rise at room temperature until double in bulk, about 45 minutes.

5. Preheat the oven to 350° (325° if using a Pyrex or dark-finish pan) 20 minutes before baking.

6. Bake in the center of the oven for 35 to 40 minutes, or until the loaves are golden brown and the bottoms sound hollow when tapped with a finger. A cake tester inserted into the center of a loaf should come out clean. Immediately remove the loaves from the pans and transfer to the racks to cool completely before slicing.

# Applesauce Bread

Makes two 9 by 5-inch loaves

¼ cup warm water (105° to 115°)

1 tablespoon (1 package) active
   dry yeast

Pinch of light brown sugar

2 cups unsweetened applesauce

1 cup warm milk (105° to 115°)

½ cup granulated sugar

4 tablespoons (½ stick) unsalted
   butter, melted

1 tablespoon salt

6 to 7 cups bread flour (depends
   on the consistency of your
   applesauce)

1 cup chopped walnuts

*Applesauce bread is a favorite quick bread, but once you try this yeasted version, you'll be hooked. French bakers have a wide repertoire of breads made with puréed and dried apples; this is a relative of that family of fruit breads. The toast is great with many kinds of jam, or try it with the Apple-Pear Butter (page 142).*

1. Place the warm water in a small bowl. Sprinkle the yeast and pinch of brown sugar over the water and stir to dissolve. Let the mixture stand until foamy, about 10 minutes.

2. Combine the applesauce, milk, granulated sugar, butter, salt, and 1½ cups of the flour in a large bowl or in the workbowl of a heavy-duty electric mixer fitted with the paddle attachment. Using a whisk or with the electric mixer on low speed, beat until smooth, about 1 minute. Add the yeast mixture and 1 cup of the flour. Beat 1 minute more, and add the walnuts. Add the remaining flour, ½ cup at a time, to form a soft dough that just clears the sides of the bowl (switch to a wooden spoon when necessary if making by hand). If the applesauce is thick and chunky, you will use the lesser amount of the flour.

3. Turn the dough out onto a lightly floured work surface and knead until smooth and springy, about 1 minute for a machine-mixed dough and 3 minutes for a hand-mixed dough. Add 1 tablespoon of flour at a time, as necessary, to prevent sticking. Place the dough in a greased deep bowl, turn once to coat the top, and cover loosely with plastic wrap. Let rise at room temperature until doubled in bulk, about 1½ hours.

4. Grease two 9 by 5-inch loaf pans. Turn the dough out onto the work surface and divide into 2 equal portions. Form each portion into a rectangular loaf. Place the loaves seam side down in the prepared pans, cover loosely with plastic wrap, and let rise at room temperature until doubled in bulk, about 45 minutes.

5. Adjust the oven rack to the lower third position and preheat the oven to 350° (325° if using a Pyrex or dark-finish pan) 20 minutes before baking.

6. Bake in the oven for 55 to 60 minutes, or until the bread is golden brown and the bottoms sound hollow when tapped with a finger. Cover loosely with a piece of aluminum foil if the tops are browning too quickly. Immediately remove the loaves from the pans and transfer to racks to cool completely before slicing.

# Raisin Bread

Makes two 9 by 5-inch loaves

¼ cup warm water (105° to 115°)

1½ tablespoons (1½ packages)
   active dry yeast

Pinch of granulated sugar

1½ cups dark raisins

1½ cups golden raisins

1 cup warm milk (105° to 115°)

1 tablespoon pure vanilla extract

¼ cup granulated sugar

¼ cup firmly packed light
   brown sugar

1 tablespoon salt

3 large eggs

4½ to 5 cups bread flour

8 tablespoons (1 stick) unsalted
   butter, at room temperature
   and cut into small pieces,
   plus 3 tablespoons, melted,
   for brushing

*Old-fashioned raisin bread, made with both dark and light raisins, is quintessential breakfast food. Dark raisins are usually sun-dried, while golden raisins are warm air–dehydrated and treated with sulfur dioxide so they do not darken from the inherent sugars that caramelize during the drying process. I like my raisin bread with loads of fruit so there are plump bursts of flavor in every bite and a pleasant "raisiny" perfume. Slice the loaf nice and thick, in at least 1-inch pieces, and serve toasted with butter and a cup of hot tea. Raisin toast is also good spread with peanut butter and a layer of cold applesauce.*

1.  Place the warm water in a small bowl. Sprinkle the yeast and pinch of granulated sugar over the water and stir to dissolve. Let the mixture stand until foamy, about 10 minutes. In another small bowl, cover the raisins with hot water and let soak at room temperature for about 2 hours, to reconstitute.

2.  Combine the milk, vanilla, granulated and brown sugars, salt, eggs, and 2 cups of the flour in a large bowl or in the workbowl of a heavy-duty electric mixer fitted with a paddle attachment. Using a whisk or with the electric mixer on low speed, beat until creamy, about 1 minute. Stir in the yeast mixture and beat for 1 minute more. Add the butter pieces and mix until incorporated. Add the remaining flour, ½ cup at a time, to form a soft, shaggy dough that just clears the sides of the bowl (switch to a wooden spoon when necessary if making by hand).

3. Turn the dough out onto a lightly floured work surface and knead until soft and springy, about 1 minute for a machine-mixed dough and 3 to 5 minutes for a hand-mixed dough. Add 1 tablespoon of flour at a time, as necessary, to prevent sticking. The dough will be smooth and springy but not dry. Place the dough into a greased deep container (such as a plastic bucket), turn once to coat the top, and cover loosely with plastic wrap. Let rise at room temperature until doubled in bulk, $1\frac{1}{2}$ to 2 hours.

4. Drain the raisins, place on a paper towel, and pat them dry. Grease the bottom and sides of two 9 by 5-inch loaf pans. Turn the dough out onto a lightly floured work surface to deflate. Pat the dough into a rough rectangle and sprinkle with the raisins. Press the raisins in. Divide the dough into 4 equal portions. With the palms of your hands, roll the dough into 4 fat, oblong sausages, each about l0 inches long. Place 2 of the pieces side by side. Starting in the center, wrap one around the other to create a fat twist effect. Repeat to form the second loaf. Place the loaves in the loaf pans and brush the tops with some of the melted butter. Cover loosely with plastic wrap and let rise at room temperature until the dough is fully doubled in bulk and no more than 1 inch over the rims of the pans, about 45 minutes.

5. Preheat the oven to 350° (325° if using a Pyrex or dark-finish pan) 20 minutes before baking.

6. Brush the tops of the loaves with the remaining melted butter. Place the pans on the center rack of the oven and bake for 40 to 45 minutes, or until the loaves are golden brown, the sides slightly pull away from the pan, and the bottoms sound hollow when tapped with a finger. Immediately remove the loaves from the pans and transfer to cooling racks.

# Oatmeal Egg Bread
# with a Cinnamon Swirl (Illustrated on page 22)

(Illustrated on page 22)

*Makes two 9 by 5-inch loaves*

2 cups boiling water

$\frac{1}{2}$ cup firmly packed dark brown sugar

2 tablespoons honey or dark corn syrup

6 tablespoons unsalted butter, at room temperature and cut into small pieces

$2\frac{1}{2}$ teaspoons salt

1 cup quick-cooking rolled oats

$\frac{1}{2}$ cup warm water (105° to 115°)

1 tablespoon (1 package) active dry yeast

Pinch of granulated sugar

$5\frac{3}{4}$ to $6\frac{1}{4}$ cups bread flour

3 large eggs

**FILLING**

$1\frac{1}{2}$ cups firmly packed light brown sugar

$2\frac{1}{2}$ tablespoons ground cinnamon or apple pie spice (see note, page 16)

4 tablespoons ($\frac{1}{2}$ stick) melted unsalted butter, for brushing

*When I make cinnamon swirl breads, I don't usually measure the brown sugar and cinnamon for the filling all that carefully. I want lots of filling so that when I have toasted slices there is some yummy melted goo oozing out. This is technically an oatmeal brioche—lots of eggs and plenty of butter. Leave the dough nice and soft; it will firm up in the refrigerator. You can also make this ahead: Prepare the dough first thing in the morning, refrigerate it for at least 8 hours, and then form the loaves and bake them in the early evening. They will be ready and waiting for your morning toast the next day.*

1. In the workbowl of a heavy-duty electric mixer fitted with the paddle attachment, combine the boiling water, brown sugar, honey, butter pieces, salt, and rolled oats. Let stand until lukewarm, 30 minutes.

2. Place the warm water in a small bowl. Sprinkle the yeast and pinch of granulated sugar over the water and stir to dissolve. Let stand at room temperature until foamy, about 10 minutes.

3. Add 2 cups of the bread flour to the oatmeal mixture. Beat on low speed until creamy, about 1 minute. Stir in the yeast mixture, eggs, and 1 cup of the flour. Beat 1 minute. Add the remaining flour, $\frac{1}{2}$ cup at a time, to form a soft, shaggy dough that just clears the sides of the bowl.

4. Turn the dough out onto a lightly floured work surface with the plastic pastry scraper and knead with the scraper (it will be too sticky to knead by hand) until soft and springy, 1 to 2 min-

utes. Add 1 tablespoon of flour at a time, as necessary, to prevent sticking. (The dough will not smooth out entirely, but will stay very soft and be slightly sticky; do not add more than the 6¼ cups of flour to try to correct this.) Place the dough into a lightly greased deep bowl. Turn the dough once to coat the top and cover loosely with plastic wrap. Let rise at room temperature until doubled in bulk, about 2 hours. Gently deflate the dough with a spatula or plastic dough scraper, cover tightly with a double layer of plastic wrap, and refrigerate overnight.

5. Grease two 9 by 5-inch loaf pans. Combine the brown sugar and spice in a medium bowl. Turn the chilled dough out onto a lightly floured work surface and divide it into 2 equal portions. Pat each portion into a rectangle about 12 by 8 inches. Brush each piece with 1½ tablespoons of the melted butter. Spread each rectangle evenly with half of the sugar and spice filling (I use my fingers to do this), leaving a 1-inch border all the way around the edge. Working from both short sides at the same time, tightly roll up each rectangle to meet in the center, forming 2 tight, scroll-like swirls. Turn the loaves over and place each in a loaf pan. Lightly brush the tops with the remaining melted butter. Cover loosely with plastic wrap and let rise at room temperature until puffy and doubled in bulk, about 1½ hours.

6. Preheat the oven to 350° (325° if using a Pyrex or dark-finish pan) 20 minutes before baking.

7. Bake on the center rack of the oven for 35 to 40 minutes, or until the loaves are golden brown and firm to the touch and a cake tester inserted into the center comes out clean. Remove the pans from the oven and let the loaves stand in the pans for 5 minutes. Remove the loaves from the pans and transfer to racks to cool completely before slicing. This bread is best at room temperature, and then reheated or toasted.

# Milk and Honey Whole Wheat Bread

Makes two 8 by 4½-inch loaves

**SPONGE**

2½ cups warm milk (105° to 115°)

2 tablespoons (2 packages) active
  dry yeast

⅔ cup honey

2 cups whole wheat flour

1 cup bread flour

**DOUGH**

⅓ cup vegetable oil

1 tablespoon salt

2 cups plus 3 tablespoons
  bread flour

2¾ cups whole wheat flour

1 egg beaten with 2 teaspoons
  water, for glaze, optional

1 tablespoon sesame seeds,
  for sprinkling, optional

*For some people, a loaf of sweet, wholesome, and nutty whole wheat bread is the epitome of a great breakfast. The secret to a moist loaf is a technique known as the sponge method, used here. By beginning with a sponge, which is done about an hour before you make the dough, all of the primary ingredients are evenly moistened and the yeast starts its work before it is mixed in and the dough is kneaded. Some bakers claim that the kneading is even easier in a loaf with a sponge starter since it moistens the gluten, which can be a bit tough in whole-grain flours.*

*You can use any sort of whole wheat flour for this recipe; a coarse grind of flour has lots of big bran flecks, which makes for a more crumbly loaf, while a fine grind yields a more even texture because the bran and germ are the same size. I like my bread sweet, but you can use half the amount of honey if you like. Keep the dough well-covered during the risings to prevent the formation of a crust, which would dry out the top of the loaf and thus restrict the delicate rising process. Serve slices topped with a layer of cottage cheese and applesauce for breakfast.*

1. To make the sponge, combine all of the ingredients for the sponge in a large bowl or in the workbowl of a heavy-duty electric mixer fitted with the whisk attachment. Using a whisk or with the electric mixer on low speed, beat until smooth, 1 minute. Scrape down the sides of the bowl with a rubber spatula and cover with plastic wrap or a fitted plastic cover. Let stand at room temperature for 1 to 2 hours. The sponge will be bubbly and have the consistency of thick, heavy cream.

2. To make the dough, gently stir the sponge down with a wooden spoon or use the paddle attachment on the electric mixer and beat on low speed for a few seconds. Add the oil, salt, and 2 cups bread flour and beat on low speed for 1 minute, until smooth. Add the whole wheat flour, $\frac{1}{2}$ cup at a time, to form a soft dough that just clears the sides of the bowl.

3. Turn the dough out onto a lightly floured work surface and knead until smooth and springy, yet slightly sticky, about 1 minute for a machine-mixed dough and 3 minutes for a hand-mixed dough. Add additional bread flour 1 tablespoon at a time, as necessary, to prevent sticking. (Do not add too much flour, as the dough must retain a definite sticky quality; this will smooth out during the rising process. The dough will also have a slightly abrasive quality due to the grind of whole wheat flour.) Place the dough in a greased deep bowl, turn once to coat the top, and cover loosely with plastic wrap. Let rise at room temperature until doubled in bulk, about 2 hours.

4. Grease two 8 by $4\frac{1}{2}$-inch loaf pans (clay pans are wonderful for this bread, giving a great crust). Turn the dough out onto the work surface and divide into 2 equal portions. Form the portions into 2 rectangular shapes (don't worry if the dough is still sticky), and place in the prepared pans. Spray the tops with butter-flavored vegetable cooking spray. Cover loosely with plastic wrap and let rise until doubled in bulk, or about 1 inch above the rims of the pans, about 1 hour.

5. Preheat the oven to 350° (325° if using a Pyrex or dark-finish pan) and place the oven rack in the lower third position 20 minutes before baking.

6. Using a serrated knife, cut 3 short diagonal gashes no deeper than $\frac{1}{4}$ inch down the length of the loaves. Brush with the egg glaze and sprinkle with the sesame seeds. Bake for 35 to 40 minutes, or until the loaves are golden brown and the bottoms sound hollow when tapped with a finger. Place a piece of aluminum foil over the tops of the loaves to control browning, if necessary. Immediately remove the loaves from the pans and transfer to racks to cool completely before slicing.

# Cornmeal Millet Bread

Makes 3 round loaves

**SPONGE**

1¼ cups warm cultured buttermilk
  (100°)

1 cup warm water (105° to 115°)

1 tablespoon (1 package) active
  dry yeast

½ cup honey

1 cup raw millet or millet meal

2 cups unbleached all-purpose flour
  or bread flour

**DOUGH**

¼ cup vegetable oil or sunflower
  seed oil

1 tablespoon salt

1½ cups yellow cornmeal

3 to 3½ cups unbleached
  all-purpose or bread flour

*Cornmeal millet bread is legendary among bread bakers. First introduced in the 1970 edition of* The Tassajara Bread Book, *there have been many incarnations of this crunchy, pale yellow bread since then. It is so good for toast that you will always want to have strawberry jam around just in case a loaf shows up (strawberries and cornmeal are a natural flavor pairing— think strawberry shortcake with a twist). It is also good as a base for Salsa-Poached Eggs with a side of Homemade Chorizo (pages 38 and 39).*

1.  To make the sponge, combine the buttermilk, water, yeast, honey, millet, and flour in a large bowl or in the workbowl of a heavy-duty electric mixer fitted with the whisk attachment. Using a whisk or with the electric mixer on low speed, beat until smooth, about 1 minute. Scrape down the sides of the bowl with a rubber spatula and cover with plastic wrap or a fitted plastic cover. Let stand at room temperature for 1 hour, or until doubled in bulk and bubbly.

2.  To make the dough, gently stir the sponge with a wooden spoon or switch to the paddle attachment if using an electric mixer and beat on low speed for a few seconds. Add the oil, salt, cornmeal, and 1 cup of the flour to the sponge and beat on low speed for 1 minute, or until smooth. Add the remaining flour, ½ cup at a time, to form a soft dough that just clears the sides of the bowl.

3.  Turn the dough out onto a lightly floured work surface and knead until smooth and springy, yet slightly sticky, about 1 minute for a machine-mixed dough and 3 minutes for a hand-

mixed dough. Add bread flour 1 tablespoon at a time, as necessary, to prevent sticking. (Do not add too much flour; the dough should be a bit soft and retain a nubby, tacky quality.) Place the dough in a greased deep bowl, turn once to coat the top, and cover loosely with plastic wrap. Let rise at room temperature until doubled in bulk, about 1½ hours.

4.  Line 2 baking sheets with parchment paper. Turn the dough out onto the work surface and divide into 3 equal portions. Form each portion into a tight, round loaf. Place the loaves seam side down on the baking sheet, cover loosely with plastic wrap, and let rise at room temperature until doubled in bulk, about 45 minutes.

5.  Preheat the oven to 350° 20 minutes before baking.

6.  Bake on the center rack of the oven for 40 to 45 minutes, or until the bread is golden brown, sounds hollow when tapped with a finger, and a cake tester inserted into the center of a loaf comes out clean. Immediately remove from the pans and transfer to racks to cool completely before slicing.

# Homemade Chorizo ❋ Serves 8

*Chorizo is a spicy chile-spiked, orange-hued Mexican sausage that comple-
ments all types of Mexican-style food. The homemade version is medium-hot
and just as flavorful as the skin-encased, long-cured version. If you can't find
the negro or ancho chile powders in a specialty foods store or ethnic market,
use more red chile powder if you wish. Be sure to mix with your hands to keep
the texture a bit coarse.*

2 pounds coarsely ground lean pork

4 large cloves garlic, pressed or minced

1 tablespoon New Mexican red chile powder

1 teaspoon negro chile powder

1 teaspoon ancho chile powder

1 ½ teaspoons ground cumin

1 teaspoon freshly ground black pepper

1 teaspoon crushed dried oregano or marjoram

½ teaspoon ground cinnamon

½ teaspoon ground cloves

½ teaspoon crushed coriander seeds

¼ cup cider vinegar

1. Combine all of the ingredients in a large bowl and mix with your hands until
   well-blended. Place in a glass container and cover tightly. Refrigerate for 24
   hours to cure.

2. Form into small patties and sauté over low heat in a skillet. The raw mixture can
   be frozen in a plastic sealable bag if you want to make it more than 3 days
   ahead.

# Salsa-Poached Eggs ❋ Serves 5

*Ever experienced the agony of poaching eggs? Weep no longer. This gem of a recipe, from food writer Victoria Wise, is foolproof. The spicy liquid is the perfect medium for keeping the eggs soft while they cook. Serve with grated cheese and more salsa or sliced tomatoes on the side.*

1½ cups medium or hot salsa fresca, puréed, or commercial salsa in a jar

¾ cup water

10 eggs

1. Combine the salsa and water in a large sauté pan. Bring to a high simmer over medium-high heat. (Use 2 smaller pans if all the eggs won't fit into one pan.)

2. When the liquid just starts to bubble, carefully crack an egg and let it slide out of the shell into the simmering salsa. Be careful not to break the yolks. Repeat this step, quickly, with all the eggs. Poach over medium-low heat 3 to 5 minutes, until the whites are firm and the yolks set. Keep an eye on the salsa, making sure it never comes to a boil.

3. Remove the eggs with a slotted spoon and place on a piece of cornmeal-millet toast. Discard the salsa and the poaching liquid.

# Seeded Dakota Bread

Makes three medium round or
two 8½ by 4½-inch loaves

2 cups warm water

½ cup cracked wheat or bulgur

2 tablespoons (2 packages) active
dry yeast

⅓ cup honey

3 tablespoons canola or
vegetable oil

2 tablespoons unsalted butter,
melted

3 tablespoons chopped walnuts

½ cup raw sunflower seeds

⅓ cup shelled raw pumpkin seeds

1 tablespoon sesame seeds

1 tablespoon poppyseeds

1 tablespoon salt

1 cup whole wheat flour

4¼ to 4¾ cups unbleached
all-purpose or bread flour

*This much-requested recipe, originally created at the Café Latte bakery in St. Paul, is what I consider the ultimate cracked wheat bread. My version of the super-satisfying bread bakes into a light, even-textured loaf, studded with nuts and seeds, that is excellent for toasting. This is a good recipe for novice bakers, despite all the extra additions.*

1.  In the workbowl of a heavy-duty electric mixer fitted with the paddle attachment, pour the warm water over the cracked wheat. Let stand for 15 minutes to soften slightly. Sprinkle the mixture with the yeast and stir in the honey. Let stand until foamy, about 10 minutes.

2.  Add the oil, butter, walnuts, sunflower, pumpkin, and sesame seeds, poppyseeds, salt, whole wheat flour, and 1 cup of the bread flour. Beat on low speed until smooth, about 1 minute. Add the remaining unbleached flour, ½ cup at a time, until a rather stiff, sticky dough is formed that just clears the sides of the bowl.

3.  Turn the dough out onto a lightly floured work surface and knead until soft and springy, about 1 minute. Add 1 tablespoon of flour at a time, as necessary, to prevent sticking. (The dough will have a nubby and slightly sticky feel. Be sure to keep this dough moist.) Place in a greased deep bowl, turn once to coat the top, and cover loosely with plastic wrap. Let rise at room temperature until doubled in bulk, about 2 to 2½ hours.

4.  Line a baking sheet with parchment paper or grease two 8½ by 4½-inch loaf pans. Turn the dough out onto the work surface. Divide into 3 equal portions for round loaves or 2 equal portions for the pan loaves. Place the round loaves on the baking sheet and the standard loaves in the loaf pans. Cover loosely with plastic wrap and let rise at room temperature until doubled in bulk, about 45 minutes.

5.  Preheat the oven to 375° (350° if using a Pyrex or dark-finish pan) 20 minutes before baking.

6.  Bake on the center rack of the oven for 35 to 40 minutes, until the bread is golden brown and the bottoms sound hollow when tapped with a finger. Immediately remove from the pans and transfer to racks to cool before slicing.

# Bagel Bread

*Makes three 9 by 5-inch loaves*

1 large russet potato (about
    12 ounces), peeled and cut into
    large chunks

2½ cups water

4 teaspoons honey, light or dark
    brown sugar, or malt syrup

4 teaspoons salt

7½ to 8 cups bread flour

1½ tablespoons (1½ packages)
    active dry yeast

¼ cup vegetable oil

3 large eggs

1 egg white, beaten until foamy
    with 1 teaspoon water, for glaze

Sesame seeds or poppyseeds
    (or half of each), for topping

*Many good bagel shops offer loaves of bagel bread alongside the different types of bagels, but the loaves disappear fast, and for good reason. The silky dough used to make bagels is outstanding baked into a loaf shape, and the bread is chewy from the potato water, just like the texture you expect in a traditionally shaped bagel. The process is much less time consuming than steaming the bagel rings, and the dough is very easy to work with because of the extra leavening power of the eggs. This is one of the first recipes I learned to make from master baker and cooking teacher Connie Pfieffer. You can vary the bread in several ways (see suggestions following recipe), each flavor rivaled by the next. Serve the bread toasted, with plenty of sweet butter and jam, melted cheese, or lox and cream cheese.*

1. To make the potato water, place the potato chunks in a small saucepan and cover with the water. Bring to a boil, lower the heat, and simmer, uncovered, until the potato is soft. Drain the potato (use the solids for another purpose, like mashed potatoes), reserving 2 cups of the potato water. Let the water cool until an instant-read thermometer reads 120°. (The potato water can be made a day ahead, refrigerated overnight, and then brought back up to temperature.)

2. To make the dough, in the workbowl of a heavy-duty electric mixer fitted with the paddle attachment, combine the potato water, honey, salt, 2 cups of the flour, the yeast, and oil. Beat on low speed until smooth, about 2 minutes. Add 1 cup more of the flour and the eggs and beat again for 2 minutes. Continue

adding the remaining flour, $\frac{1}{2}$ cup at a time, to form a soft dough that just clears the sides of the bowl.

3. Turn the dough out onto a lightly floured work surface and knead until smooth, firm, and springy, about 2 minutes. Add 1 tablespoon of flour at a time, as necessary, to prevent sticking. Place in an oiled deep bowl, turn once to coat the top, and cover loosely with plastic wrap. Let rise at room temperature until doubled in bulk, 1 to $1\frac{1}{2}$ hours.

4. Brush three 9 by 5-inch loaf pans with oil. Turn out the dough onto a lightly floured work surface and divide into 3 equal portions. Form into rectangular loaves and place in the prepared pans. Cover loosely with plastic wrap and let rise at room temperature only until level with the tops of the pans, about 45 minutes (these loaves will rise a lot in the oven).

5. Preheat the oven to 375° (350° if using a Pyrex or dark-finish pan) 20 minutes before baking.

6. Gently brush the tops with the egg glaze and sprinkle with the topping. Bake on the center rack of the oven for 40 to 45 minutes, until crusty, golden brown, and the bottoms sound hollow when tapped with a finger. Remove from the pans and transfer to racks to cool completely before slicing.

*(continued)*

## Whole Wheat Bagel Bread

Substitute 3 cups regular or white whole wheat flour for an equal portion of the bread flour.

## Pumpernickel-Rye Bagel Bread

Substitute 2 cups dark rye flour for an equal portion of unbleached flour. Add $\frac{1}{4}$ cup molasses, 1 tablespoon unsweetened cocoa, 1 tablespoon powdered instant coffee, and 2 tablespoons cornmeal. Sprinkle the tops with caraway seeds and coarse salt after glazing.

## Onion Bagel Bread

Sauté 1 onion, finely diced, in 3 tablespoons vegetable oil until limp (or use rehydrated dry onion flakes). Set aside. Halfway through baking, remove the loaves from the oven and brush the tops with a second coating of the egg glaze. Immediately spread the onion mixture over each loaf and return the loaves to the oven to finish baking.

## Cinnamon-Raisin Bagel Bread

Use $\frac{1}{4}$ cup of sugar instead of honey and add 1 tablespoon ground cinnamon, 1 teaspoon ground mace or nutmeg, and $\frac{1}{2}$ teaspoon ground cardamom with the flour in the initial mixing of the dough. Add 2 cups dark or golden raisins during the mixing of the dough. Sprinkle with sesame seeds after glazing.

# English Muffin Batter Bread

*While I love English muffins, sometimes I just don't have time to make them. This yeasted batter bread is the answer. It is easy to make and produces a round loaf that slices into pieces that look very much like an English muffin. The taste is exactly the same, and when toasted, the crunch is unmistakable.*

1. Place the warm water in a small bowl. Sprinkle the yeast and pinch of the sugar over the water and stir to dissolve. Let the mixture stand until foamy, about 10 minutes.

2. In the workbowl of a heavy-duty electric mixer fitted with the paddle attachment, combine the milk, the remaining sugar, egg, oil, salt, and 1½ cups of the flour. Beat for 1 minute on medium speed, until thick and sticky. Add the yeast and baking soda mixtures and beat for 1 minute more. Continue to add the remaining flour, ½ cup at a time, on low speed and beat on medium speed for about 2 minutes. The batter will be sticky like soft dough. Scrape down the sides with a rubber spatula.

3. Generously grease the bottom and sides of three 4½-inch-diameter glass baking canisters or two 13-ounce coffee cans with butter and sprinkle generously with the cornmeal or farina, coating all of the surfaces by turning the mold. Divide the batter evenly between the two molds, filling each half full. Use a rubber spatula to push the batter into the corners, and smooth the top with flour-dusted fingers. Cover loosely with plastic wrap greased with nonstick vegetable cooking spray and let rise at room temperature until doubled in bulk, about 45 minutes to 1 hour, or until the batter is even with the rim of the pans and slightly lifting the plastic wrap. Do not let the dough rise to more than double.

*(continued)*

½ cup warm water (105° to 115°)

4 teaspoons active dry yeast

Pinch of sugar

1¼ cups milk

2 tablespoons sugar

1 large egg

2 tablespoons vegetable oil or unsalted butter, melted

2 teaspoons salt

4¾ cups unbleached all-purpose flour

½ teaspoon baking soda dissolved in 1 tablespoon cold water

Yellow cornmeal or farina, for dusting pans

4. Twenty minutes before baking, place the oven rack in the lower third position and preheat the oven to 350° (325° if using the glass molds).

5. Bake in the oven 40 to 45 minutes, or until the tops are crusty and dark brown and sound hollow when tapped with a finger, and a cake tester inserted into the center comes out clean. An instant-read thermometer should read 200°. Expect the dome to rise 2 to 3 inches above the rim of the can.

6. Remove the loaves from the oven and cool in the pan for 5 minutes. Turn the pans on their sides and slide the loaves out onto a rack to cool on their sides for at least 2 hours. Slice in thick rounds, toast, and serve with lots of sweet butter and some Cranberry-Lime Curd (page 148). To store, wrap in a resealable plastic bag at room temperature for up to 3 days or in the freezer for up to 2 months.

# Baked Tomato French Toast ✳ *Makes 6 servings*

*French toast is just as good savory as well as sweet—maybe even better—and a great way to feed a group. The bread is layered with Canadian bacon, cheese, and tomatoes. This is a memorable brunch entrée.*

10 to 12 slices (1 loaf) white or country bread, crusts removed, cut in ½-inch-thick slices

3 tablespoons olive oil

12 slices Canadian bacon (about 8 ounces)

2 cups shredded Cheddar or Monterey Jack cheese

8 large eggs

3 cups milk (or undiluted evaporated skim milk)

Salt and freshly ground black pepper

3 large tomatoes (about 1½ pounds), cored and cut into 4 thick slices

⅓ cup grated Parmesan cheese, for sprinkling

1. Preheat the oven to 350°. Arrange the bread on a 10 by 15 by 1-inch baking sheet; it is okay to cut them to fit, just make sure they touch each other. Brush each slice of bread on both sides with some of the olive oil. Layer the bacon over the bread and sprinkle the Cheddar cheese over the top.

2. Place the eggs and milk in a large bowl and beat using a whisk or handheld immersion blender, until foamy. Season with salt and pepper (keep in mind that the bacon is somewhat salty). Pour the milk mixture over the bread.

3. Bake on the center rack of the oven for 10 minutes. Remove the pan from the oven and place the tomato slices over the top in a single layer. Sprinkle the Parmesan cheese over the tomatoes and bake for 15 minutes more, or until the custard is set. Cut into squares and serve immediately.

# Spinach and Jack Breakfast Strata ❉ Makes 8 generous servings

*Leftover bread is great for making some spectacular brunch dishes, like this savory bread pudding. Strata is a culinary term coined in the 1950s for an old-fashioned casserole composed of layered ingredients. It uses the same technique as for constructing a lasagne, only bread is the main starch. The results are spectacular, and stratas are a real convenience food, as they are assembled up to 12 hours ahead and refrigerated until baking just before serving for brunch with fresh fruit and muffins. This is my mom's strata, served to overnight guests. She learned it from Liz Tiger, an excellent cook and mother of Mike Tiger, one of the defense lawyers in the Oklahoma City bombing trial, and decades ago, defending the Chicago Seven.*

1 small loaf firm, day-old white or egg bread, sliced thin and crusts trimmed

2 ½ cups shredded mild Cheddar cheese

2 ½ cups shredded Monterey Jack cheese

1 (7-ounce) can diced roasted green chiles

8 ounces bacon, cooked, drained, and crumbled, or cooked chicken apple sausages, casings removed

1 (10-ounce) package frozen chopped spinach, defrosted and squeezed dry

1 yellow onion, chopped

3 cups milk

4 large eggs

1. Generously grease a 9 by 13-inch shallow baking dish. Arrange half of the bread slices, slightly overlapping, in the bottom of the casserole. Toss the cheeses together in a medium bowl. Sprinkle half of the cheese over the bread. Arrange a layer of all of the green chiles on the top of the cheese, and then a layer of all of the bacon or sausage, and then all of the spinach and all of the onion. Sprinkle with the rest of the cheese and top with a layer of the bread slices to cover the filling completely.

2. Using a whisk, beat together the milk and eggs in a medium bowl. Slowly pour the mixture over the bread. Gently press the top bread down to soak it with the milk mixture. Cover tightly with aluminum foil and refrigerate overnight.

3. When ready to bake, preheat the oven to 350°. Bake on the center rack of the oven, uncovered, for 1 hour, or until the center is puffed and golden, and a knife inserted into the center comes out clean. Let stand for 15 minutes before serving hot.

# Blueberry French Toast   ✳  *Makes 8 servings*

*I used to make a blueberry bread pudding for brunches but have recently opted to make this French toast instead. Both syrup and sauce can be made a day ahead and gently reheated before serving, or you can serve the French toast with a good-quality maple syrup.*

12 (1-inch) slices Buttermilk White Bread (page 24), ends trimmed off
   and cut into cubes

2 (8-ounce) packages cream cheese, cold, and cut into 1-inch cubes

1 pint fresh blueberries

12 large eggs

⅓ cup maple syrup

2 cups whole milk

Freshly grated nutmeg, to taste

1. Grease a 9 by 13-inch glass baking pan. Place half of the bread cubes in the pan. Scatter all of the cream cheese over the bread. Sprinkle with the blueberries and arrange the remaining bread cubes on top, creating layers.

2. In a large bowl, blend the eggs, maple syrup, and milk using a whisk or hand-held immersion blender. Pour over the bread in the pan and sprinkle with the nutmeg. Cover with aluminum foil and refrigerate for 2 hours, or overnight.

3. Preheat the oven to 350°. Bake on the center rack of the oven, covered with the foil, for 30 minutes. Remove the foil and bake until puffed and golden brown, 30 minutes more. Serve warm, right from the pan, with blueberry syrup and lemon sauce on the side, or with maple syrup.

## Blueberry Syrup ❋ *Makes about 2 cups*

1 cup sugar

2 tablespoons cornstarch

1 cup water

1 ½ cups fresh blueberries, rinsed and drained

2 tablespoons unsalted butter

Combine the sugar and cornstarch in a medium saucepan and add the water. Stir constantly with a whisk over medium-high heat until the mixture comes to a full boil. Add the blueberries, reduce the heat to medium, and continue to cook until the syrup thickens, becomes clear, and the berries burst. Remove the pan from the heat and stir in the butter. Serve warm.

## Lemon Sauce ❋ *Makes about 1⅓ cups*

¼ cup freshly squeezed lemon juice

½ cup water

½ cup sugar

Grated zest of 2 lemons

1 tablespoon cornstarch

3 tablespoons unsalted butter

Combine the lemon juice, ¼ cup of the water, the sugar, and zest in a small saucepan. Warm over low heat just until sugar is dissolved. Dissolve the cornstarch in the remaining ¼ cup water and pour into hot lemon mixture. Stir constantly with a whisk over medium-high heat until the mixture comes to a full boil, thickens, and becomes clear, about 3 minutes. Remove from the heat and stir in the butter. Serve warm or at room temperature.

# Sunday Breakfast: Pancakes and Waffles

Pancake and waffle lovers rejoice! Whether you like them small or large, dense or fluffy, crisp or soft textured, there's a stack to suit just about any appetite. These popular—and healthy—comfort foods don't need to be limited to weekend enjoyment. They can be a cherished part of morning menus any day of the week. The ingredients are easy to keep on hand, and the recipes are easy to mix and bake. They take advantage of an array of healthy whole grains—oatmeal and whole wheat are a few favorites—and are rich in wholesome complex carbohydrates, while being deeply satisfying. To create an effortless breakfast, whip together a variety of baking mixes before you need them, or just mix up a fresh batch when the mood strikes you.

Pancakes are known by many names—hotcakes, griddlecakes, hoecakes, flapjacks, silver dollars, string-of-flats, flannel cakes—depending on where you are and the size of the cooked pancake. They fall into two categories: thin batters baked either in an oven or on the stovetop, and thicker batters dropped by spoonfuls onto a hot, oiled griddle heated on a stovetop (or even a camp stove!). The pancake batters in this chapter are constructed just like a muffin batter—the wet and dry ingredients are first mixed separately, and then right before baking, both mixtures are combined by hand with a minimum of

*Raised Waffles (page 61)*

strokes, rather than with an electric mixer, to form a range of thick to thin batters. Never overmix; these batters are versatile, but delicate!

One-quarter cup batter is the general rule for a medium 4-inch, round pancake; 2 tablespoons will give a dollar size; and ½ cup makes large, plate-sized rounds. You can oil the griddle with an oil-soaked paper towel or with a pat of cold butter quickly run over the top of the hot surface. The batter is gently poured onto a greased and well-heated griddle (heat electric models to 375°) using a measuring cup or large spoon held just above the surface of the griddle. Let the batter spread out by itself—you want to take care not to disturb the delicate bubbles created by the leavening—and leave enough room between each cake so they don't touch while baking. Never try to rearrange the pancakes while the first side is baking or they won't bake evenly. Remember that pancakes are baked, never fried, and are not tossed into the air, but rather are gently turned to keep the precious air bubbles intact.

Waffles use a similar batter but they cook in an enclosed griddle, which bakes both sides at the same time. The waffle iron stamps the waffle with the familiar grid pattern, so perfect for pools of melted butter and syrup to collect. Electric models are the most common type of waffle iron. Hinged models dating back to medieval Europe for baking over an open fire or on top of wood-burning stoves are beloved collector's items. Waffle batters generally have a bit more fat in the recipe than pancakes. The fat gives waffles their characteristic light brown color and crispness. Use butter for a crisper waffle and oil for a more tender one. Yeast waffles need a controlled liquid temperature to allow the yeast to grow and an overnight rising to develop the batter texture, so you'll need to plan ahead for these.

One waffle usually requires ¾ to 1 cup of batter, depending on the size of your waffle iron. Avoid overfilling the grids; excess batter will spill out when you close the lid. High temperatures create a crisp waffle, lower temperatures make moister ones. Bake it until there is no more steam and the waffle is evenly brown (you'll have to peek unless you have that wonderful little light indicator). Remove the waffle from the iron with a fork to protect your fingers.

There is no way around it—pancakes and waffles cool off fast. How do you keep them warm while you prepare batch after batch? It's easy. Hold them in a 200° oven on a baking sheet covered with a clean kitchen towel until you are ready to serve. (Many cooks heat their serving plates at the same time.)

There are a number of toppings beyond the ambrosial 100% maple syrup, all of which should be made ahead or assembled before baking. With a bit of forethought, you—the *real* waffle maker—won't end up stuck in the kitchen while everyone else is feasting.

Whether you're making pancakes or waffles, finish baking off an entire batter. If there are any uneaten pancakes or waffles, you can store them in plastic freezer bags and freeze them for up to 2 months. The frozen waffle is ready to be popped in the toaster, emerging as crisp as the day it was made, and the pancakes will be as soft and steamy after a short stint in the microwave as they were the day they came off the hot griddle.

# American Silver Dollar Pancakes

*Makes about eighteen 3-inch pancakes*

2 cups unbleached all-purpose flour

2 tablespoons yellow cornmeal

1 tablespoon baking powder

2 teaspoons baking soda

½ teaspoon salt

2 large eggs

2 cups cultured buttermilk

5 tablespoons vegetable oil or canola oil

*I clipped this recipe from a* Gourmet *magazine, dated November 1958, that I picked up at a garage sale. It was a requested recipe from the newly opened Pancake Palace, a restaurant at the San Francisco International Airport that served all sorts of pancakes to hungry travelers. You don't hear much about silver dollars these days, but when I was a kid it was a big deal to get a newly minted silver dollar for your birthday. The "dollar," a mainstay on griddles out West during the gold rush, is a unique size for a pancake, a bit smaller than the regular breakfast hotcake, but every bit as satisfying. Make an overlapping pile and serve with butter and plenty of real maple syrup.*

1.  Combine the flour, cornmeal, baking powder, baking soda, and salt in a mixing bowl. In another bowl, beat the eggs until light and fluffy, about 1 minute, and whisk in the buttermilk. Make a well in the center of the dry ingredients and pour the buttermilk mixture and the oil into the center. Stir until just until combined; do not overmix. The batter will have small lumps.

2.  Heat a griddle or heavy skillet over medium heat until a drop of water skates over the surface, and lightly grease. Using a large, oversized spoon (mine measures 1¾ tablespoons) for each pancake, spoon the batter onto the griddle, fitting as many as possible on the griddle with a few inches in between. Cook until bubbles form on the surface, the edges are dry, and the bottoms are golden brown, about 1 minute. Turn once, cooking the opposite sides until golden, 30 to 45 seconds. Serve immediately, or keep warm in a 200° oven until ready to serve.

# Margaret's Oatmeal Hotcakes

*This delightful recipe came from my friend Margaret, who is eighty-eight years old at this writing. A great baker, she loves to mix the oatmeal and buttermilk the night before and then stir in the rest of the ingredients in the morning. No mess, no fuss. While she favors dried cranberries or chopped dried apricots in the batter, I have also used hunks of chopped fresh banana in the winter or giant fresh boysenberries in the summer. I freeze any leftover pancakes in heavy-duty plastic freezer bags; they reheat perfectly in the microwave. Serve with the butter and maple syrup warmed together so that the butter is already melted.*

1. Mix together the buttermilk and oats in a medium bowl (I use one with a plastic lid). Refrigerate overnight.

2. In the morning, remove the mixture from the refrigerator. Sprinkle the flours and sugar over the oats. Add the eggs, oil, baking powder, baking soda, and salt and whisk into the oatmeal mixture. The batter will be thick; thin it with a little more buttermilk, if you like. Stir in the cranberries or apricots.

3. Heat a griddle or heavy skillet over medium heat until a drop of water skates over the surface, and lightly grease. Using a 1/4-cup measure for each pancake, ladle the batter onto the griddle. Cook until bubbles form on the surface, the edges are dry, and the bottoms are golden brown, about 2 minutes. Turn once, cooking the until golden, about 1 minute. Serve immediately, or keep warm in a 200° oven until ready to serve.

4. To make the warm pancake syrup, combine the maple syrup, butter, and rum in a small saucepan or microwave-proof bowl. Heat slowly until the butter is melted. Serve immediately.

## Makes about 1 dozen 4-inch pancakes

2 cups cultured buttermilk

1 3/4 cups quick-cooking rolled oats

1/4 cup unbleached all-purpose flour or white spelt flour

1/4 cup whole wheat pastry flour

2 tablespoons firmly packed light or dark brown sugar

2 large eggs, beaten

1/4 cup light olive oil

1 teaspoon baking powder

1 teaspoon baking soda

1/3 teaspoon salt

1 cup dried cranberries or chopped dried apricots (or a combination of the two)

### WARM MAPLE PANCAKE SYRUP

1 cup pure maple syrup

6 tablespoons (3/4 stick) unsalted butter

1 tablespoon golden rum (optional)

# Lemon Yogurt Pancakes with Dried Fruit Compote

Makes about twenty 4-inch pancakes

## DRIED FRUIT COMPOTE

1 (8-ounce) package dried apricots, chopped

1 (8-ounce) package dried figs, stemmed and chopped

¼ cup dried cherries

4 cups unsweetened apple juice

2 whole cinnamon sticks

¼ cup firmly packed light or dark brown sugar

## PANCAKE BATTER

2 cups unbleached all-purpose flour

¼ cup brown rice flour

2 tablespoons sugar

1 teaspoon baking powder

¾ teaspoon baking soda

½ teaspoon salt

2 large eggs

1⅓ cups cultured buttermilk

1 (8-ounce) carton lemon yogurt

Grated zest of 1 large lemon

¼ cup freshly squeezed lemon juice

3 tablespoons unsalted butter, melted

*For decades I had a beautiful lemon tree outside my kitchen door, so I had the bright yellow citrus fruit available year-round. I couldn't find enough ways to use their delightful tangy, tart flavor. Serve this dried fruit compote to drip down the golden stack, or try the cakes with a homemade Blueberry Syrup (page 51).*

1. To make the compote, place the dried apricots, figs, and cherries, apple juice, and cinnamon sticks in a large bowl and cover tightly with plastic wrap or a plastic lid. Refrigerate overnight.

2. In the morning, place the mixture in a medium saucepan with the brown sugar. Bring to a boil, decrease heat to low, and simmer for 10 to 15 minutes, uncovered. The mixture will be thick and hot. Remove the pan from the heat, discard the cinnamon sticks, and cool to room temperature before serving.

3. Combine the flours, sugar, baking powder, baking soda, and salt in a medium bowl. In another medium bowl, beat the eggs with a whisk until light and fluffy, about 30 seconds. Whisk in the buttermilk, yogurt, zest, and lemon juice. Make a well in the center of the dry ingredients and pour the buttermilk mixture and the melted butter into the center, stirring just until combined. The batter will be thick and delicate.

4. Heat a griddle or heavy skillet over medium heat, and lightly grease. For each cake, spoon ¼ cup of the batter onto the griddle, leaving a few inches in between. Cook until bubbles form on the surface, the edges are dry, and the bottoms are golden brown, about 1 minute. Turn once, cooking the opposite sides until golden, 30 to 45 seconds. Serve immediately, topped with the compote, or keep warm in a 200° oven until ready to serve.

# Blueberry Pancakes

*Buttermilk is the favored liquid for making pancakes because it creates a delicious and light cake. And with blueberries... well, what can I say. If I left out a recipe for these, I would be remiss. I make my pancakes with lots of fresh berries or berries I stash in the freezer for just this purpose. Serve these with pure maple syrup and whipped sweet butter dripping down the sides.*

Makes eighteen 4-inch pancakes

1⅓ cups unbleached all-purpose flour

⅓ cup brown rice flour

1 tablespoon baking powder

1 teaspoon baking soda

½ teaspoon salt

2 cups cultured buttermilk

3 large eggs

¼ cup vegetable oil

½ teaspoon pure vanilla extract

1 pint fresh or drained canned blueberries, or 1 (12-ounce) package unsweetened, unthawed frozen blueberries

1. Combine the all-purpose and brown rice flours, baking powder, baking soda, and salt in a medium mixing bowl. In another medium bowl, whisk together the buttermilk, eggs, oil, and vanilla. Add the buttermilk mixture to the dry ingredients, stirring just until combined; do not overmix. The batter will have small lumps and be thick. Let the batter stand at room temperature for 15 minutes.

2. Heat a griddle or heavy skillet over medium heat until a drop of water skates over the surface, and lightly grease. Using a ¼-cup measure for each pancake, ladle the batter onto the griddle. Sprinkle each pancake with 6 or 7 whole berries. Cook until bubbles form on the surface, the edges are dry, and the bottoms are golden brown, about 2 minutes. Turn once, cooking the opposite sides until golden, about 30 seconds. Serve immediately, or keep warm in a 200° oven until ready to serve.

# My Best Buttermilk Waffles

Makes 6 to 8 large waffles,
depending on iron size

1 ¼ cups unbleached all-purpose
flour

¼ cup whole wheat flour

3 tablespoons firmly packed light
brown sugar

1 heaping tablespoon yellow cornmeal or polenta (I use one that is
a combination of cornmeal and
buckwheat)

¼ teaspoon baking powder

1 teaspoon baking soda

½ teaspoon salt

3 large eggs, separated

2 tablespoons unsalted butter or
margarine, melted

1 ¼ cups cultured buttermilk

*I use a Vitantonio waffle maker imported from Italy. It costs no
more than American brands and is a wonderful piece of equipment. I don't suffer for it not having a nonstick surface, I just
spray it with nonstick vegetable cooking spray before heating.
It has become seasoned with use, which also helps. Serve these
waffles with bowls of sliced fresh strawberries, warm applesauce, and a mix of equal parts of sour cream and plain yogurt
to pile on top.*

1. Heat the waffle iron to medium-high or according to manufacturer's instructions. In a large bowl, combine the all-purpose
and whole wheat flours, brown sugar, cornmeal, baking powder, baking soda, and salt.

2. In a separate bowl, using an electric mixer, beat the egg whites
until stiff peaks form.

3. Make a well in the center of the dry ingredients and add the egg
yolks, melted butter, and buttermilk, stirring just until moistened
and smooth. Fold in the beaten egg whites with a spatula.

4. Brush the waffle iron grids with oil or melted butter. Pour
about ¼ cup of the batter into the center of the iron. Close the
lid and bake until the waffle is crisp and well browned, about
4 to 5 minutes. Remove the waffle from the iron with a fork to
protect your fingers. Serve immediately, keep warm in a 200°
oven until ready to serve, or cool completely on racks, store in
plastic bags, and freeze for up to 2 months.

# Raised Waffles (Illustrated on page 52)

*In the 1980s, John Hudspeth opened a breakfast restaurant called Bridge Creek down the street from Chez Panisse in Berkeley. I would eat there every time I was in town, savoring their crisp waffles doused in maple syrup. They were unlike any I had ever tasted, and I yearned for the recipe. The menu consultant, I learned, was Marian Cunningham, local author of the revised editions of the* Fannie Farmer Cookbook, *and it turns out the waffles are a Fannie Farmer standard from 1896. Yeasted waffles are not as common as their quick cousins, but the time needed for mixing is the same, and an overnight rest creates a spectacular waffle that is ready to bake first thing in the morning. My version uses a bit of brown rice flour.*

1. The night before serving, place the warm water in a large bowl or deep plastic container (the batter will double as it sits overnight). Sprinkle with the yeast and let stand for 5 minutes to dissolve and become bubbly.

2. Add the milk, melted butter, salt, sugar, and all-purpose and brown rice flours, and beat with a whisk until smooth, about 1 minute. Cover with plastic and refrigerate overnight.

3. In the morning, heat the waffle iron to medium-high or according to manufacturer's instructions. Brush the waffle iron grids with oil. Add the eggs, baking soda, and baking powder into the batter and beat with a whisk until evenly incorporated. Ladle 1/3 cup batter into the center of the iron. Close the lid, and bake until the waffle is crisp and golden, about 2 minutes. Remove the waffle from the iron with a fork to protect your fingers. Serve immediately, or keep warm in a 200° oven until ready to serve. Leftover batter can be refrigerated in a tightly covered container for up to 2 days.

Makes about 8 waffles, depending on iron size

1/2 cup warm water

2 1/2 teaspoons active dry yeast, or 2 teaspoons SAF fast-acting yeast

2 cups tepid milk (about 100°)

8 tablespoons (1 stick) unsalted butter, melted

1 teaspoon salt

1 teaspoon sugar

1 3/4 cups unbleached all-purpose flour

1/4 cup brown rice flour

2 large eggs

1/4 teaspoon baking soda

1/4 teaspoon baking powder

# Peanut Butter Waffles

*Makes about 6 large waffles, depending on iron size*

2 cups unbleached all-purpose flour

2 tablespoons baking powder

1 tablespoon firmly packed light brown sugar

¼ teaspoon salt

2 large eggs

4 tablespoons (½ stick) unsalted butter or margarine, melted

⅔ cup creamy or crunchy peanut butter

1¾ cups milk

1 banana, diced

*Peanut butter has had a dedicated following since it was introduced as a health food at the St. Louis World's Fair in 1890. I find that peanut butter waffles get an enthusiastic response from the youngest to the oldest diners. It is not an overpowering ingredient in these waffles, and it goes perfectly with maple syrup. If you refrigerate your peanut butter, bring it to room temperature before mixing the batter or you will have a blob that is hard to mix. I personally use the chunky style.*

1. Heat the waffle iron to medium-high, or according to manufacturer's instructions. In a large bowl, combine the flour, baking powder, brown sugar, and salt.

2. In a separate bowl, using a whisk or with an electric mixer on low speed, beat the eggs, butter, peanut butter, and milk until foamy, about 1 minute. Pour the peanut butter-milk mixture into the dry ingredients, stirring just until moistened and smooth. Fold in the diced banana.

3. Brush the waffle iron grids with oil or melted butter. Pour about ¼ cup of the batter into the center of the iron. Close the lid and bake until the waffle is crisp and well browned, about 4 to 5 minutes. Remove the waffle from the iron with a fork to protect your fingers. Serve immediately, keep warm in a 200° oven until ready to serve, or cool completely on racks, store in plastic bags, and freeze for up to 2 months.

# Easy Italian Popover Puff

2 tablespoons olive oil

1 tablespoon butter

2 large eggs

1 cup milk

¾ cup unbleached all-purpose flour

1 tablespoon yellow cornmeal
   or polenta

¼ teaspoon salt

½ cup shredded mozzarella cheese

¼ cup shredded provolone cheese

3 cups Salsa di Pomodoro (recipe
   follows) or store-bought Italian
   marinara sauce

Freshly grated Parmesan cheese,
   for sprinkling

*A baked pancake calls for a thin batter that is baked in the oven instead of on top of the stove. It's one big puff that looks and tastes like an oversized popover. This savory version, served with a flavorful tomato sauce and melted Italian cheeses, is very popular because it is easy and quick to assemble and ready to serve hungry diners in 40 minutes. Serve it right out of the oven while it's still puffed in the pan (it will collapse as it cools) with Canadian bacon and a fresh fruit salad. Don't wait for company to make this!*

1.  Preheat the oven to 400° (375° if using a Pyrex or dark-finish pan). Place the olive oil and butter in a 9-inch Pyrex or ceramic pie plate. Place on the center rack of the hot oven to melt the butter and warm the oil.

2.  Meanwhile, in a small bowl using a whisk or a handheld immersion blender, or in a food processor fitted with the metal blade, beat the eggs until foamy, about 30 seconds. Add the milk, flour, cornmeal, and salt. Beat until smooth and foamy, about 30 seconds more.

3.  Using oven mitts, carefully remove the hot pan from the oven. Slowly pour the batter over the warmed oil. The pan will be half full. Return the pan to the oven and bake for 25 minutes, until puffy and well-browned. Remove from the oven and sprinkle with the shredded cheeses. Bake 5 minutes more to melt the cheeses. Cut into wedges, ladle some hot salsa or marinara sauce over the top, put a bowl of Parmesan cheese on the table, and serve immediately.

# Salsa di Pomodoro ❋ Makes 3 cups

*This is an excellent, simple, all-purpose Italian tomato sauce. I love the unortho-dox addition of the corn kernels, which complements the tomato.*

1 large shallot, chopped

¼ cup extra-virgin olive oil

1 (28-ounce) can plum tomatoes, packed in purée

3 tablespoons dry red wine, such as Merlot

5 or 6 chopped fresh basil leaves, or 2 teaspoons dried Italian herb blend

Salt and freshly ground black pepper, to taste

1 cup fresh or undefrosted frozen baby yellow corn kernels (about 1 ear)

1. In a medium saucepan, sauté the shallot briefly over medium heat in the oil. Add the tomatoes with their liquid, wine, basil, and salt and pepper. Bring to a boil, and then decrease the heat to low. Simmer, uncovered, for 30 minutes.

2. Add the corn and cook for 5 to 10 minutes more. The sauce can be stored in a tightly covered container in the refrigerator for up to 5 days and in the freezer for up to 1 month.

# German Puff Pancakes with Apple Compote and Bourbon Pecan Butter

Serves 8

**BOURBON PECAN BUTTER**

8 tablespoons (1 stick) unsalted butter, at room temperature

1½ tablespoons finely chopped pecans

1½ tablespoons pecan oil, optional

1 tablespoon bourbon

**APPLE COMPOTE**

6 tablespoons unsalted butter

5 tart cooking apples, such as Granny Smith or Fuji, peeled, cored, and sliced ¼ inch thick

⅓ cup sugar, or to taste

Juice of 1 large lemon

1 teaspoon ground cinnamon

½ teaspoon freshly grated nutmeg

½ teaspoon ground allspice

⅔ cup dried cranberries

**PANCAKE BATTER**

4 tablespoons unsalted butter, cut into 8 equal portions

6 large eggs

1¼ cups milk

1¼ cups unbleached all-purpose flour

½ teaspoon salt

*For those mornings when a scone and coffee is just not enough, here is a sweet version of the German puff pancake, also called a Dutch baby, baked in individual soufflé dishes for a dramatic, glamorous presentation. You can make the apple compote and the pecan bourbon butter the night before. Serve alongside crisp bacon or browned chicken-apple breakfast sausages.*

1. To make the pecan butter, put all of the ingredients for the butter in a medium bowl and mash together with a fork until evenly blended. Refrigerate, covered, until ready to serve.

2. To make the apple compote, melt the butter in a large skillet. Add the apples and cook over medium-high heat for 1 minute. Add the sugar, lemon juice, and spices and stir to coat the apples. Add the dried cranberries and cook for 1 minute, until a syrup forms and the apples are tender when pierced with a fork. Do not overcook or the apples will become mushy.

3. Preheat the oven to 425°. Place a piece of butter in each of 8 (8-ounce) soufflé dishes. Place the dishes on a baking sheet on the center rack of the oven to melt the butter.

4. Meanwhile, in a mixing bowl, using a whisk or a handheld immersion blender, or in food processor fitted with the metal blade, beat the eggs until foamy, about 30 seconds. Add the milk, flour, and salt, and beat until smooth and foamy, 30 seconds more.

5. Using oven mitts, carefully remove the hot baking sheet from the oven. Pour $\frac{1}{2}$ cup of the batter into each soufflé dish. Immediately return the pan to the oven and bake for 10 minutes, until puffy. Lower the oven temperature to 375° and bake for 5 minutes more.

6. Remove the pan from the oven and place each soufflé dish on a serving plate lined with a doily. Divide the bourbon pecan butter into 8 equal portions and place a pat on the top of each puffed pancake, letting it melt into the center and down the sides. The puff pancakes can be eaten out of the soufflé dish or turned out onto a plate by loosening the sides and bottom with a spatula. Serve immediately with the bowl of apple compote on the side to spoon into the center of the pancake.

# Sweet Rolls:
# The Perfect Morning Fare

A well-made sweet roll is a great accomplishment for the home baker. Sweet rolls are technically considered coffee cakes, as they typically use the same yeast dough as a coffee cake; but rather than being served in a pan or mold, sweet rolls are preportioned into individual servings. Sweet rolls are synonymous with the sweet spice cinnamon; in fact, cinnamon and sticky buns both have their origin in the *schnecken* ("snail"), Germany's rolled and filled sweet roll. You will often see a reference to Philadelphia sticky buns, since the cinnamon roll was a fixture in restaurants in that city during the nineteenth century. The word "bun" comes from the Old French *bugne*, or "swelling," which these single-serving breads do as they rise in the oven.

Whatever their shape, sweet rolls have a crossover appeal: One look at one, much less one bite of one, will bring the child out in any adult. I have included some rolls in this chapter that are not swirled: the cinnamon breadsticks, which are more crunchy; the English tea-table staple known as the crumpet, which looks like a round sponge; a soft, sweet breakfast pretzel; and the baking powder–risen donut, the roll with a hole. I also give you the fastest homemade croissant ever, made with brioche dough, and a fruit-filled pocket.

*Giant Macadamia Nut Cinnamon Rolls (page 75)*

## The Fastest Cinnamon Rolls

*Makes 12 rolls*

¾ cup dried cherries, blueberries,
cranberries, golden raisins,
or chopped prunes

Boiling water to cover

DOUGH

¾ cup cottage cheese

⅓ cup sugar

⅓ cup cultured buttermilk

4 tablespoons (½ stick) unsalted
butter, melted, plus 2 tablespoons, for brushing

1½ teaspoons pure vanilla extract

2 cups unbleached all-purpose flour

1 tablespoon baking powder

¼ teaspoon baking soda

½ teaspoon salt

FILLING

⅔ cup firmly packed light
brown sugar

½ cup firmly packed dark sugar

1¼ teaspoons ground cinnamon

1 teaspoon ground allspice

¼ teaspoon ground cloves

VANILLA ICING

⅔ cup confectioners' sugar, sifted

3 to 4 teaspoons cold cultured
buttermilk

1 teaspoon pure vanilla extract

*This is a very unusual cinnamon roll. It is made with baking powder and cottage cheese and mixed as if it were a quick biscuit dough. The result is a cinnamon roll that is more firm to the bite than one made with yeast. I found a number of recipes for cottage cheese baking in a German cookbook, and they call this type of baking blitz, or quick. If yeast baking is at all intimidating to you, this is the perfect recipe to wow your breakfast set. The rolls are best eaten warm the day they are baked.*

1. Preheat the oven to 400°. Grease a 9-inch square or round baking pan. Set aside. Place the dried fruit in a small bowl and pour the boiling water over. Cover and set aside.

2. Place the cottage cheese, sugar, buttermilk, 4 tablespoons melted butter, and vanilla in the bowl of a food processor fitted with the metal blade and process until smooth. Add the flour, baking powder, baking soda, and salt to the workbowl and pulse until the dough clumps like a biscuit dough, 8 to 10 pulses. Turn the dough out onto a lightly floured work surface and knead gently, folding the dough over and pushing away from you 4 to 5 times, until the dough is smooth. Do not overwork the dough. Using a rolling pin, roll out the dough to make a 12 by 15-inch rectangle. Brush the entire surface with the 2 tablespoons melted butter, leaving a ½-inch border around all the edges.

3. To make the filling, combine the sugars, cinnamon, allspice, and cloves in a medium bowl and sprinkle over the surface of the dough. Pat to press the sugar into the surface. Drain the dried fruit and pat dry with a paper towel. Distribute the fruit over the sugar mixture.

4. Starting at the long edge, roll up the dough jelly-roll fashion. Pinch the seam to seal, leaving the ends open. With a sharp knife, cut the roll into 12 equal pieces. Set the rolls cut side up, showing the spiral design, in the baking pan.

5. Place immediately on the center rack of the oven and bake for 25 to 30 minutes, or until golden brown and firm to the touch. Remove the pan from the oven and run a metal spatula around the edges of the rolls. Lift the rolls out of the pan one at a time and place them right side up on a wire rack positioned over a plate or a piece of waxed paper.

6. To glaze, place the ingredients for the icing in a small bowl or 2-cup liquid measuring cup (the spout makes pouring easy). Using a small wire whisk, beat until smooth and a thick, pourable consistency. Adjust the consistency with additional drops of buttermilk. Drizzle the icing in a zigzag pattern over each roll. Let the rolls stand for at least 15 minutes before serving.

## DOUGH

1¼ cups warm water
  (105° to 115°)

2 tablespoons (2 packages) active
  dry yeast

½ cup granulated sugar

1¼ cups warm cultured buttermilk
  (105° to 115°)

3 large eggs

½ cup vegetable oil

1 tablespoon salt

About 8½ cups unbleached
  all-purpose flour

## CARAMEL GLAZE

1 cup firmly packed light
  brown sugar

1 cup firmly packed dark
  brown sugar

Pinch of salt

1 cup heavy whipping cream

¼ cup light corn syrup

## CINNAMON FILLING

1 cup granulated sugar

½ cup firmly packed light
  brown sugar

2½ tablespoons ground cinnamon

12 tablespoons (1½ sticks) unsalted
  butter, at room temperature

1 cup chopped pecans

1 cup dried currants or dried
  cranberries

# Caramel Breakfast Rolls

*I can't believe I found this lovely recipe on the back of my package of cheesecloth! Caramel rolls are the first sweet roll I ever made. Very elegant, they are known as pan rolls, as they are baked in a small pan and then pulled apart to serve. This is a nice, big recipe for fluffy, sweet rolls, perfect for serving at brunches. The recipe does not call for any melting of the sugar; all you have to do is mix up the cream and brown sugar. The glazing happens on its own in the oven. Imagine the delight of working with caramel, one of the more mystical components of a baker's kitchen, and ending up with perfectly glazed rolls! Make sure to serve the rolls slightly warm and not directly from the oven, to avoid burning your mouth on the hot glaze. The rolls can be made a day ahead, wrapped in plastic, stored in the refrigerator, and warmed before serving. For longer storage, cover in plastic wrap and then in a layer of aluminum foil and freeze for up to 6 weeks.*

1. Place ½ cup of the warm water in a small bowl. Sprinkle the yeast and a pinch of the sugar over the water and stir to dissolve. Let the mixture stand until foamy, about 10 minutes.

2. Combine the remaining water, the remaining sugar, and the buttermilk, eggs, oil, salt, and 2 cups of the flour in a large bowl or in the workbowl of a heavy-duty electric mixer fitted with a paddle attachment. Using a whisk or with the electric mixer on low speed, beat until creamy, about 1 minute. Add in the yeast mixture and beat a few seconds. Add the remaining flour, ½ cup at a time, until a soft, shaggy dough that just

clears the sides of the bowl is formed (switch to a wooden spoon, when necessary, if making by hand).

3. Using a plastic pastry scraper, turn the dough out onto a lightly floured work surface and knead by hand until soft and springy, about 1 minute for a machine-mixed dough and 3 minutes for a hand-mixed dough. Add 1 tablespoon of flour at a time, as necessary, to prevent sticking. Keep the dough nice and soft, yet at the same time, smooth and springy.

4. Place the dough into a lightly greased, deep plastic container. Turn the dough once to coat the top, and cover with plastic wrap. Let rise at room temperature until doubled in bulk, about $1\frac{1}{4}$ hours.

5. Meanwhile, prepare the caramel glaze and the filling. To make the glaze, grease the sides and bottom of two 9 by 13-inch Pyrex or metal baking pans. Place the sugars, salt, cream, and corn syrup (the corn syrup helps the sugars melt properly) in a small bowl and stir with a wooden spoon until smooth. Using a rubber spatula, spread half of the mixture evenly over the bottom of each prepared pan. Set aside. To start the filling, in a small bowl, combine the sugars and cinnamon and set aside.

6. Turn the dough out onto a lightly floured work surface and divide into 2 equal portions. Roll or pat each portion into a 12 by 15-inch rectangle. Leaving a 1-inch border around the edges of the rectangle, spread the surface with half of the soft butter, and then sprinkle evenly with half of the sugar-cinnamon mixture, all of the pecans, and the currants or cranberries, in that order. Roll up jelly-roll fashion, starting from the long edge, and pinch the bottom seam to seal, to make a long log. Using a serrated bread knife in a gentle sawing motion, cut each log into 12 equal pieces, $1\frac{1}{4}$ inches thick. Place the slices close together in the baking pans, with the spiral cut side facing up; each pan will have 3 rolls down and 4 rolls across. Cover loosely with plastic wrap and let the rolls rise at room temperature for 45 minutes, or until puffy and even with the rims of the pans.

*(continued)*

(Before this last rise, the rolls can be refrigerated for 2 to 24 hours or frozen for up to 2 weeks, retarding the dough for bake-off at a later time. To refrigerate, cover the pans loosely with plastic wrap and refrigerate for 2 to 24 hours. Remove the pans from the refrigerator and let rest at room temperature for 30 minutes before baking. To freeze, use disposable aluminum pans covered with a layer of plastic wrap, then aluminum foil, to avoid freezer burn or breakage. When ready to thaw and bake off the rolls, remove them from the freezer and let stand, uncovered, at room temperature until doubled in bulk, about 6 hours, or for 24 hours in the refrigerator, covered, and then an additional 30 minutes at room temperature; proceed with recipe.)

7. Preheat the oven to 350° (325° if using Pyrex or dark-finish baking pans) 20 minutes before baking. Cover 2 baking sheets with parchment.

8. Bake the rolls on the center rack of the oven for 35 to 40 minutes, or until the tops are brown (the two pans will easily fit in most ovens; if they don't, bake one pan at a time). If the center rolls don't seem done, cover the top loosely with foil and bake another 5 to 8 minutes. Remove the pans from the oven and let stand for 5 minutes on wire racks. Place a rack on top of each pan and, securely holding the hot pan with oven mitts, invert the pans and then slide onto the baking sheets. Take care not to touch the hot caramel while you are working. Using a metal spatula, scrape out any caramel left in the pan and place it on top of the rolls. Let the rolls cool for at least 20 minutes, and then pull them apart to serve slightly warm.

# Giant Macadamia Nut Cinnamon Rolls

(Illustrated on page 68)

*Giant cinnamon rolls are an irresistible, homey morning treat and are often filling enough to be the main course. These particular rolls are made all the more special by the macadamia nut–raisin filling and the orange icing that will have you smacking your lips. I was delighted to learn that macadamia nuts are the healthiest nut you can eat, having a one-to-one ratio of omega-3 to omega-6 fatty acids, making the nut oil even lower in saturated fat and healthier for your heart than olive oil. The Hawaiian nut orchards must be thriving—a tree does not produce for fifteen years, but thereafter has about five harvests a year—since unsalted macadamias are now available in bins in my supermarket. Be sure to keep the dough nice and soft so the rolls are easy to fill and roll up into a spiral. The nuts and raisins are an accent to the filling, rather than being dominant, so don't worry if they look sparse when you make the filling. The rolls are placed on the baking sheet without touching so they can flatten out into a large round during baking. I give instructions for shapes other than the freestanding swirl if you like to experiment with different-looking sweet rolls—flowers, twin snails, fans—all just a cut, twist, or slash away.*

1. Place the warm water in a small bowl. Sprinkle the yeast and pinch of brown sugar over the water and stir to dissolve. Let the mixture stand until foamy, about 10 minutes.

2. Combine the buttermilk, sugar, eggs, salt, and 2 cups of the flour in a large bowl or in the workbool of a heavy-duty electric mixer fitted with the paddle attachment. Using a whisk or with

*(continued)*

Makes 16 rolls

### DOUGH

$2/3$ cup warm water (105° to 110°)

2 tablespoons (2 packages) active dry yeast

Pinch of light brown sugar

$1 1/2$ cups tepid cultured buttermilk (100°)

$1/4$ cup firmly packed light brown sugar

2 large eggs

1 tablespoon salt

7 to $7 1/2$ cups unbleached all-purpose flour

4 tablespoons ($1/2$ stick) unsalted butter or margarine, at room temperature

### FILLING

4 tablespoons ($1/2$ stick) unsalted butter, melted

$1 1/2$ cups light brown sugar

3 tablespoons ground cinnamon

$1 1/2$ cups chopped unsalted macadamia nuts

$3/4$ cup golden raisins

### ORANGE ICING

4 tablespoons ($1/2$ stick) unsalted butter, at room temperature

2 cups sifted confectioners' sugar

1 teaspoon pure vanilla extract

$1/2$ teaspoon almond extract

$1/4$ to $1/3$ cup freshly squeezed orange juice

the electric mixer on low, beat for 1 minute more. Add the soft butter and yeast mixture. Beat another minute. Add the remaining flour, $\frac{1}{2}$ cup at a time, until a soft dough that just clears the sides of the bowl is formed (switch to a wooden spoon, when necessary, if making by hand).

3. Turn the dough out onto a lightly floured work surface and knead until smooth and springy, 3 to 5 minutes. Add 1 tablespoon of flour at a time, as necessary, to prevent sticking. The dough will be soft. Place in a greased deep bowl and cover loosely with plastic wrap. Let rise at room temperature until doubled in bulk, about $1\frac{1}{2}$ hours.

4. Line 2 large baking sheets with parchment paper. Turn the dough out onto the work surface; do not knead. With a rolling pin, roll out the dough into a large 14 by 20-inch rectangle. For the filling, brush the surface with the melted butter and sprinkle evenly with layers of the brown sugar, cinnamon, nuts, and raisins. Roll up from the long edge, jelly-roll fashion. Pinch the seam to seal and leave the ends open.

   To cut the rolls, use a sharp chef's knife. To create plain, swirled rolls, use the knife in a gentle back and forth motion, slicing 16 slices about $1\frac{1}{2}$ inch thick.

   To create flowers, mark the top of each cut slice into 3 equal portions about $\frac{1}{2}$ inch thick. Make the first two cuts about three-quarters of the way through the roll. Make the third cut completely through, severing it from the two connected sections. Fan out the two connected sections and lay the third separate section on top of the cut, lying off to the side, so that there are 3 overlapping sections of swirl.

   To create twin snails, cut each slice in half about three-quarters of the way through the roll. Lay the slices open and twist them in the center at the connected section of dough, turning one slice upside down. Both slices will have the swirl pattern facing up.

   To create fans, cut the roll into 8 equal portions about $2\frac{1}{2}$ inches thick. Place on the baking sheets, cut sides facing up. Make 3 or 4 cuts three-quarters of the way through the roll (keep all of the sections connected at the bottom), and gently fan the slices.

Place each roll at least 3 inches apart on the baking sheets. Cover loosely with a clean kitchen towel and let rise at room temperature until doubled in bulk, about 45 minutes to 1 hour.

5. Preheat the oven to 350° 20 minutes before baking.

6. Bake on the center rack of the oven for 18 to 25 minutes (the fans will take the longest to bake). Do not overbake, as the rolls dry out easily during reheating.

7. While the rolls are baking, make the orange icing: Place all of the ingredients for the icing in a large bowl or in the workbowl of a heavy-duty electric mixer. Beat on low speed until light and fluffy, about 1 minute. The icing should be the spreading consistency of a thick buttercream frosting.

8. Remove the rolls from the oven and, using a small metal spatula, immediately frost each one with a layer of icing. Serve the rolls warm, or let cool completely and place the rolls in resealable plastic freezer bags and freeze for up to 2 months. To reheat, remove the rolls from the freezer and let thaw in the bag at room temperature. Remove the rolls from the bag, place on a heatproof plate, and microwave on high for no more than 30 seconds to warm, or bake at 350° for 5 to 7 minutes. Serve immediately.

# Challah Fruit Pockets

*Makes about 40 pockets*

½ cup warm water (105° to 115°)

1 tablespoon (1 package) active
   dry yeast

Pinch of sugar

8 tablespoons (1 stick) unsalted
   butter, at room temperature

⅓ cup sugar

2 large eggs

½ cup milk

½ cup sour cream

1 teaspoon salt

4 to 4½ cups unbleached
   all-purpose flour

**FILLING**

Prune Lekvar, Poppyseed Paste
   (recipes follow), or Apricot
   Butter (page 144)

Hamantaschen *are individual filled cakes, most notably baked as gifts during the Jewish holiday of Purim in the spring. But they are so delectable, I like to make them at any time of year. The German word* taschen *translates to "pocket," but the shape is more triangular, as three sides are pulled up and pinched together at the top. The prune lekvar is my favorite filling and the traditional one, but a thick poppyseed paste or Apricot Butter filling (page 144) are also nice. Supermarkets carry the Solo brand of all three flavors, or you can make your own. Each filling recipe is enough for one batch of dough. These fruit pockets are good accompaniments to tea and coffee, and are a delight for late evening snacking.*

1. Place the warm water in a small bowl. Sprinkle the yeast and pinch of sugar over the water and stir to dissolve. Let the mixture stand until foamy, about 10 minutes.

2. Place the butter and sugar in a large bowl or in the workbowl of a heavy-duty electric mixer fitted with the paddle attachment. Using a whisk or with the electric mixer on low speed, cream the butter and sugar until light and fluffy, about 1 minute. Separate 1 egg, reserving the white in the refrigerator. Add the whole egg and the yolk to the creamed mixture. Gradually add the yeast mixture, the milk, sour cream, salt, and 2 cups of the flour; beat hard until creamy, 2 minutes. Add the remaining unbleached flour, ½ cup at a time, until a soft dough is formed that just clears the sides of the bowl (switch to a wooden spoon, when necessary, if making by hand).

3. Turn out the dough onto a well-floured work surface and knead a few times just to smooth the dough. Add 1 tablespoon of flour at a time, as necessary, to prevent sticking. The dough will be very soft. Place in a greased deep bowl and cover loosely with plastic wrap. Let rise at room temperature until doubled in bulk, about 2 hours. (The dough can be refrigerated to rise overnight at this point.)

4. Line 2 large baking sheets with parchment paper. Turn out the dough onto a lightly floured work surface. Divide in half and roll each portion out into a large 16-inch round about ¼ inch thick. Cut the dough into 3-inch rounds using a biscuit cutter or a clean 6-ounce tuna fish can with both ends removed. Place 1 heaping teaspoon of the desired filling in the center of each circle. Combine the reserved egg white with a teaspoon of water and beat until foamy. Brush the edges of the dough with the egg white. Bring 3 side flaps of the circle up to meet in the center to form a triangle and pinch tightly at the tip. Place the pockets on the baking sheets 1 inch apart. Repeat with the remaining section of dough, rerolling the scraps. Cover the baking sheets loosely with plastic wrap and let rest at room temperature for 20 to 30 minutes, until puffy.

5. Preheat the oven to 350° 20 minutes before baking.

6. Bake one pan at a time on the center rack of the oven for 15 minutes, or until golden brown. Using a metal spatula, remove the pockets from the pans and transfer to wire racks to cool.

## Prune Lekvar ❋ *Makes about 2¼ cups*

**3 cups (about 18 ounces) dried pitted prunes**

**1½ teaspoons ground cinnamon**

**1 cup water**

**1 tablespoon freshly squeezed lemon juice**

**1 teaspoon grated lemon zest**

In a small saucepan, combine the prunes, cinnamon, and water. Bring to a boil, and then cover and lower the heat to medium low. Simmer until soft, about 10 minutes. Remove the pan from the heat. Add the lemon juice and zest and cool slightly to room temperature. Purée the mixture until smooth in a food processor fitted with the metal blade or push through a food mill. Use immediately, or store in a covered container in the refrigerator.

## Poppyseed Paste ❋ *Makes about 2 cups*

**1½ cups black or blue poppyseeds**

**¾ cup milk**

**½ cup honey**

**⅓ cup currants**

**3 tablespoons unsalted butter**

**1½ teaspoons almond extract**

Place the poppyseeds in a medium bowl and pour boiling water over, to cover. Soak for 1 to 2 hours. Drain well through a fine-mesh sieve, and combine with the milk in another medium bowl. Place in a blender or food processor fitted with the metal blade and process until the poppyseeds are as fine as possible. Place in a small saucepan and add the honey. Bring to a boil and then lower the heat to medium low. Simmer until thick, about 10 minutes. Stir in the currants, butter, and almond extract. Let cool, and then store in the refrigerator for up to 3 days. The mixture should be used chilled.

# Hungarian Poppyseed Rolls

*This Hungarian poppyseed sweet bread roll, known formally as* Mákos es Dios Kalacs, *is called* beigli *in village slang and* strucla *in Poland. It is a tremendously popular sweet dough that is rolled around a cooked poppyseed filling, much like a strudel, and made for spring and winter holidays. Every home baker has a recipe. My Aunt Marge remembers helping my grandmother make these rolls, and this is the closest I could come to her recipe, which was never written down. I especially like to use white spelt flour for an authentic, delicate flavor, since it was the main flour used in Europe during the Middle Ages and spelt is a favored crop in Hungary today. I love to make the egg glaze with instant espresso; it gives an intense, shiny brown finish to the roll. You can grind the poppyseeds yourself with a poppyseed grinder (available from King Arthur catalog, imported from Eastern Europe), or buy them already ground. Using ground poppyseeds is a must, as the processing extracts the tasty, starchy center of the seed and yields a smooth filling rather than a gritty one. As an alternative, use canned poppyseed filling, available in most supermarkets (you will need 1½ cans). Serve a tray of sliced rolls, cut on the diagonal, with a cup of good coffee laced with Cognac after brunch.*

1. Put ⅓ cup of the warm milk in a small bowl. Sprinkle the yeast and pinch of sugar over the top and stir to dissolve. Let the mixture stand until foamy, about 10 minutes

2. Put the butter and sugar in a large bowl or in the workbowl of a heavy-duty electric mixer fitted with the paddle attachment.

*(continued)*

1 cup warm milk (105° to 115°)

1 tablespoon (1 package) active
   dry yeast

Pinch of sugar

8 tablespoons (1 stick) unsalted
   butter or margarine, at room
   temperature

½ cup sugar

1 large egg plus 1 egg yolk

3 tablespoons sour cream

1 teaspoon pure vanilla extract

½ teaspoon salt

4 to 4½ cups unbleached all-
   purpose flour, white spelt flour,
   or white whole wheat flour

## POPPYSEED FILLING

1 cup black poppyseeds, ground

1¾ cups half-and-half

¼ cup sugar

¼ cup honey

2 teaspoons almond extract

¼ cup cornstarch

1 large egg yolk

1 cup golden raisins

3 tablespoons Amaretto, brandy,
   or Cognac

1 whole egg, beaten with
   ¼ teaspoon powdered instant
   espresso, for glaze

Using a whisk or with the electric mixer on low speed, cream until light and fluffy, about 1 minute. Add the egg and egg yolk and sour cream and beat for 1 minute. Beat in the remaining ⅔ cup milk, the yeast mixture, the vanilla, salt, and 1 cup of the flour. Add the remaining flour, ½ cup at a time, until a soft dough is formed that just clears the sides of the bowl (switch to a wooden spoon when necessary if making by hand).

3. Turn out the dough onto a lightly floured work surface and knead until smooth and pliable, about 1 minute for a machine-mixed dough and 3 minutes for a hand-mixed dough. Add 1 tablespoon of flour at a time, as necessary, to prevent sticking. The dough will be very soft but not sticky. Place in a greased deep bowl, turn once to coat the top, and cover loosely with plastic wrap. Let rise at cool room temperature for 4 to 6 hours, or as long as overnight in the refrigerator, deflating once or twice by poking into the center of the dough with your finger.

4. While the dough is rising, prepare the poppyseed filling. In a small saucepan, combine the ground poppyseeds and 1¼ cups of the half-and-half. Bring to a boil. Lower the heat and simmer, uncovered, for 10 minutes, stirring occasionally, until slightly thickened. Halfway into the simmering time, stir in the sugar, honey, and almond extract with a whisk. Using a whisk or a food processor fitted with the metal blade, blend the cornstarch and egg yolk with the remaining ½ cup half-and-half, until smooth. Using a whisk, gradually add the cornstarch mixture to the simmering poppyseed mixture, stirring constantly over medium heat until it thickens. When the whisk becomes clogged, switch to a wooden spoon or rubber spatula. The filling should clear the sides and bottom of the pan as it is being stirred. Cook 1 minute more, stirring constantly. Remove from the heat and, with a spatula, scrape into a small bowl to cool completely at room temperature. Cover tightly with plastic wrap to refrigerate. Makes about 2¾ cups.

5. Toss the golden raisins and liqueur together in a small bowl and macerate for at least 30 minutes. (If made a day ahead, store, covered, in the refrigerator until ready to use.)

6. Grease a large baking sheet. Turn the dough out onto the work surface and divide into 4 equal portions. Pat each portion into a thick 6 by 4-inch rectangle, set on the baking sheet, cover loosely with a clean kitchen towel, and let rest for 30 minutes.

7. Cut four 12-inch pieces of parchment paper and grease with butter. Using a floured rolling pin on a clean or very lightly floured work surface to minimize sticking, roll or pat out each dough portion into a rectangle about 12 by 9 by ¼ inches thick. Evenly spread the surface of each portion with one-quarter (about ⅔ cup) of the poppyseed filling and sprinkle some of the macerated raisins over the top. Working with 1 rectangle at a time and starting from the long edge, fold over in 2-inch sections. Continue to fold the dough in this manner to create a flattish oval (rather than round) log of dough. Pinch the seams together and tuck under at the ends. Brush each roll with the egg glaze and prick all over with a fork. Puncture the rolls down the middle, every 3 inches, with an ice pick or a large meat fork to prevent bursting. Place a sheet of the greased parchment on the work surface and set a roll on the bottom end; roll up loosely, leaving the ends open. Place the 4 rolls, seam side down, horizontally on the baking sheet. Let rest, uncovered, at room temperature until doubled in bulk, about 45 minutes.

8. Preheat the oven to 350° 20 minutes before baking.

9. Bake on the center rack of the oven until golden, 40 to 45 minutes. The rolled parchment causes the dough to expand out the ends, instead of being short and puffy, forming a long, elegant, baguette-style loaf.

10. Remove the pan from the oven and carefully unroll each loaf, discarding the parchment. Let the loaves rest on the baking sheet for 10 minutes. Using a large metal spatula, transfer the loaves to a rack to cool completely. Handle the hot breads carefully, as they are quite delicate. Cut into thin slices with a serrated knife to serve. Store, wrapped in plastic, in the refrigerator.

# Glazed Orange Morning Rolls

Makes 24 rolls

½ cup warm water (105° to 115°)

1 tablespoon (1 package) active
    dry yeast

½ cup sugar

1¼ cups warm milk (105° to 115°)

8 tablespoons (1 stick) unsalted
    butter or margarine, melted

2 large eggs

2 teaspoons salt

5½ to 6 cups unbleached
    all-purpose or bread flour

## CITRUS FILLING

12 tablespoons (1½ sticks) unsalted
    butter or margarine, softened

1½ cups sugar

Grated zest of 2 lemons and
    1 orange

*I discovered this recipe in the 1970s. It was originally made with the filling rolled up inside a crescent shape. While the buns were incredibly delicious, the filling poured out during baking, which not only made a mess, but deprived the buns of their tasty, tangy center. I decided to make them in muffins tins so the precious filling would become a glaze as it melted. The result is perfection.*

1. Put the water in a small bowl and sprinkle the yeast and a pinch of the sugar over the top. Stir to dissolve and let stand until foamy, about 10 minutes.

2. Combine the milk, the remaining sugar, the melted butter, eggs, salt, and 1½ cups of the flour in a large bowl or in the work-bowl of a heavy-duty electric mixer fitted with the paddle attachment. Using a whisk or with the electric mixer on low speed, beat until smooth, about 1 minute. Add the yeast mixture and 1 cup flour and beat for 1 minute more. Add the remaining flour, ½ cup at a time, to form a soft dough that just clears the sides of the bowl (switch to a wooden spoon when necessary if making by hand).

3. Turn the dough out onto a lightly floured work surface and knead until smooth and springy, 1 minute for a machine-mixed dough and 2 to 3 minutes for a hand-mixed dough. Add 1 tablespoon of flour at a time, as necessary, to prevent sticking. The dough will be very soft, but not sticky. Place in a greased deep bowl, turn once to coat the top, and cover loosely with plastic wrap. Let rise at room temperature until doubled in bulk, about 1½ hours.

4.  To make the citrus filling, using a fork or an electric mixer on low speed, cream the butter, sugar, and zests until smooth. Set aside at room temperature. (You want a spreadable consistency.)

5.  Grease 2 standard 2¾-inch muffin tins. Gently deflate the dough by turning it out onto a lightly floured work surface. Roll out with a rolling pin into a 12 by 26-inch rectangle about ½ inch thick. Spread the surface of the rectangle evenly with the citrus filling, leaving a 1-inch border around the edges. Roll up jelly-roll fashion, from the long end. Using a serrated knife or a length of dental floss, cut the roll crosswise into 24 equal portions 1 to 1¼ inches thick. Pull the end flap of dough around to cover the spiral on one cut surface; this will be the bottom. Place each roll in a muffin cup and press gently to flatten each swirl slightly to completely fill the cup. Repeat the shaping for each roll. Cover loosely with plastic wrap and let rise at room temperature for about 45 minutes, until puffy and 1 inch above the rim of the pan. (The unbaked rolls may be refrigerated at this point to rise overnight and transferred from the refrigerator directly to the preheated oven in the morning.)

6.  Preheat the oven to 375° 20 minutes before baking.

7.  Place the muffin tins on an aluminum-foil-covered baking sheet to catch any overflowing filling. Bake on the center rack of the oven until golden brown, 25 to 30 minutes. Invert the muffin tins to remove the buns and cool, glazed side up, on a wire rack set over a piece of parchment or waxed paper to catch the drips. Let stand until just warm before serving, or let cool completely and freeze in individual freezer bags for up to 1 month.

# Crumpets

Makes fifteen 3 1/2- to 4-inch crumpets

1 tablespoon (1 package) active
    dry yeast

Pinch of sugar

1 cup warm water (105° to 115°)

1 1/2 cups warm milk (105° to 115°)

2 tablespoons unsalted butter,
    melted, or vegetable oil

1 1/2 cups unbleached
    all-purpose flour

1 1/2 cups bread flour

1/4 teaspoon cream of tartar

1 1/2 teaspoons salt

1/2 teaspoon baking soda

*A crumpet is a breakfast bread par excellence. Native to the British Isles, its preparations and traits vary from England to Scotland to Wales. Crumpets are not as bready as an English muffin, but are moist, full of air holes, and light textured. They are made from a yeasted pancake batter and are formed when the batter is poured into metal rings that mold them while they bake on a hot griddle. A crumpet batter that is baked without the mold is known as a* pikelet.

*It is important that the crumpet batter is the right consistency to achieve the right texture and characteristic mass of air pockets. Be prepared for a batter that is very wet (a crumpet with no holes is described as "blind"). For cooking, I use my tortilla griddle, but you can use a cast-iron or regular (not non-stick) pancake griddle. I keep a stack of metal molds that I made by cutting out the top and bottom from 6-ounce tuna cans; they work great even though they are a bit smaller than true crumpet rings. Crumpets are not split in half to eat. Instead, you just slather butter and jam all over the honeycombed surface after toasting or when they are hot off the griddle.*

1. In a large mixing bowl or in the workbowl of a heavy-duty electric mixer fitted with the paddle attachment, sprinkle the yeast and the sugar over 1/2 cup of the warm water. Stir to dissolve and let stand until foamy, about 10 minutes.

2. Add the milk, butter, and unbleached flour to the yeast mixture. Beat vigorously with a large whisk or with the electric mixer on low speed until creamy, about 2 minutes. Add 1/2 cup of the bread flour and the cream of tartar and beat for 3 min-

utes. Add the remaining bread flour, $\frac{1}{3}$ cup at a time. You will have a smooth, thick batter (switch to a wooden spoon when necessary if making by hand). Cover the bowl loosely with plastic wrap and let stand at room temperature until doubled in bulk, about 1 hour. The batter will have the appearance of being just about to break along the top surface.

3. Sprinkle the salt over the surface of the batter and beat to deflate, about 1 minute. In a 1-cup liquid measuring cup, stir together the reserved $\frac{1}{2}$ cup warm water and the baking soda. Gently stir into the batter for about 30 seconds. Cover again with the plastic wrap and let rest for 30 minutes.

4. Preheat an electric griddle to 375°, or heat a cast-iron or pancake stovetop griddle over medium-high heat until a drop of water sprinkled on the griddle skates across the surface. Your hand will feel very warm when held $1\frac{1}{2}$ inches over the griddle for 20 to 30 seconds. Lightly grease the surface with a piece of butter held with a piece of paper towel. Grease the insides of as many ring molds as will fit on your griddle (usually 3 or 4 per batch) and place them on the griddle; it is okay if their sides touch. Let them heat for 20 seconds. (If you pour the batter into a cold ring, the crumpet will stick.)

5. Ladle $\frac{1}{3}$ cup of batter into each ring, filling the mold with about $\frac{1}{2}$ inch of batter. (You don't want the crumpets to be too thick.) The batter will bubble as it heats up. If the batter is too thin and runs out of the mold, add a few tablespoons of flour into the batter in the bowl; if there are no bubbles, thin with a few tablespoons of water. Reduce the heat to medium and cook the crumpets for 8 to 9 minutes. The crumpets will hold their own shape, be covered with bubbles, and the surface will appear dry.

6. Using a kitchen towel and holding 2 sides of the mold, ease the mold up and off the crumpet. Using a thin metal cake spatula or a metal pancake turner, flip each crumpet over. Cook the holey side for 2 to 3 minutes, until it turns pale golden. The top side will be smooth and light brown. Transfer the crumpets to a rack to cool, or place in a cloth-lined basket to keep warm to serve immediately. Wipe off the griddle with a paper towel and repeat the process with the remaining batter, regreasing and heating the rings before filling each time. Store in plastic bags at room temperature.

# Cake Donuts

Makes 24 donuts, plus 24 donut holes

3 cups unbleached all-purpose flour (can be half whole wheat flour)

1 cup cake flour

1 tablespoon baking powder

1 tablespoon vanilla powder

1 teaspoon ground nutmeg or cardamom

½ teaspoon baking soda

¾ teaspoon salt

1 large whole egg plus 2 egg yolks

1 cup sugar (can be half light brown sugar, which is especially good if you are making whole wheat donuts)

3 tablespoons butter or margarine, melted

⅓ cup sour cream

1 cup cultured buttermilk

½ teaspoon pure vanilla extract

About 1 quart vegetable oil, for deep frying

*Little breads with a hole in the center are among some of the world's oldest morning foods made throughout the world. The fried donut that we now consume in America is the descendant of the* olykoek, *which came to the New World with the first Dutch settlers. My boyfriend, Steve, and I used to enjoy plain cake donuts—our favorite because of their cakelike texture and not-too-sweet flavor—with cups of plain ol' brewed coffee (in the days before designer coffee shops) at the local donut shop. Perched on bar stools, we'd survey the different types of donuts while we dunked the freshly made donuts in our coffee, sometimes making a bit of a soggy mess and drinking the soaked crumbs with the last sips in the cup. Years later, I found a great donut shop in Santa Cruz, California, that made the same cake donuts, but as a whole wheat version. The plebeian donut was out of fashion during the croissant, muffin, and scone crazes, but I notice it is back with a splash, with newspapers reporting lines of people snaking out the door waiting to buy their donuts. You can drizzle these with a maple or chocolate icing (and then sprinkle with coconut, chopped nuts, or colored jimmies) or dredge in cinnamon sugar or powdered sugar, favorites with children; but I like them plain.*

1. In a medium bowl, stir together the all-purpose and cake flours, baking powder, vanilla powder, nutmeg, baking soda, and salt.

2. In the workbowl of a heavy-duty electric mixer, cream the egg, yolks, and sugar on low speed until thick and lemon colored,

about 1 minute. Add the melted butter and sour cream and beat on medium speed for 30 seconds. On low speed, add the dry ingredients in 3 separate additions, alternating with the buttermilk and vanilla extract. The dough will be very soft. Cover the bowl and refrigerate for 2 hours. This chilling before frying prevents the dough from absorbing too much oil while the donuts cook.

3. Using a large rubber spatula or a plastic dough card, scrape the dough out of the bowl onto a lightly floured work surface. Knead a few times, like for biscuit dough, just until it holds together, and keeping it as soft as possible. With a rolling pin, quickly roll out the dough to a thickness of $\frac{1}{2}$ inch (the donuts will puff during frying). Do not add too much flour or over-handle at this point or the donuts will be tough. Using a $2\frac{3}{4}$-inch donut cutter or two smooth-edged biscuit cutters, one large and one small (to make the hole) dipped in flour, cut out the donuts.

4. In a deep heavy 4-quart Dutch oven, wok, or portable electric deep-fat fryer, pour the vegetable oil to a depth of 2 inches. Using a deep-fry thermometer, heat to 375° (I do this while I am rolling and cutting out the donuts so that the dough does not warm up). Place a clean brown paper bag or a few layers of paper towels on a baking sheet at the side of the stove for draining the donuts. Carefully test the oil by dropping in a leftover scrap of dough; the oil is hot enough when it puffs immediately. Carefully slide 2 or 3 pieces of dough (don't forget the holes) off a metal pancake turner into the hot oil. It is important not to crowd them. Turn a few times with a large slotted metal spoon when the donut rises to the surface; cook until golden brown, about 2 minutes per side (1 minute for the holes). Remove with the slotted spoon to drain, and cool to room temperature.

# Chocolate Glaze ✳ Enough for 21 cake donuts

1 ½ ounces (1 ½ squares) unsweetened or bittersweet chocolate

2 tablespoons unsalted butter

1 ½ cups sifted confectioners' sugar

Pinch of powdered espresso powder or instant coffee granules

¼ teaspoon pure vanilla extract

1 tablespoon boiling water

1. In the top of a double boiler, melt the chocolate and butter over simmering water.

2. In a small bowl, place the confectioners' sugar and coffee. Pour in the melted chocolate and vanilla. Using a whisk, beat well until smooth. Adjust the consistency of the glaze by adding boiling water a few drops at a time, just enough to keep the glaze spreadable.

3. Using a small metal spatula, spread the glaze on the top of each donut, letting some run down the sides. Let stand until cool and the glaze hardens.

# Cinnamon Sugar ✳ Enough for 1 batch of cake donuts

1 cup granulated sugar

2 ½ teaspoons ground cinnamon, or to taste

1. Place the sugar and cinnamon in the bowl of a food processor fitted with the metal blade and process for 15 seconds.

2. Pour the cinnamon-sugar into a clean brown paper bag (a lunch sack is great). Drain the fried donuts for 1 minute, and then, while still warm, place one at a time while still warm in the paper bag and gently shake to coat with the mixture. Remove from the bag and cool.

# Brioche Pretzels

Makes 12 large pretzels

4½ cups unbleached all-purpose flour (exact measure)

1 tablespoon (1 package) active dry yeast

¼ cup sugar

2 teaspoons salt

½ cup warm milk

5 large eggs, at room temperature

1 cup (2 sticks) unsalted butter, at room temperature, cut into small pieces

1 egg beaten with 1 tablespoon milk, for glaze

⅓ cup turbinado (raw) or Demerara sugar, for sprinkling

*Once I saw a picture of a specialty food gift basket from Fauchon food emporium in Paris. Peeking out of the top of the laden basket was an oversized pretzel. After some research, I found out that it was not a bread pretzel, but a brioche pretzel, glazed with coarse sugar crystals. In conversation with food doyenne Madeleine Kamman, I asked her about this soft pretzel made with brioche egg dough. "Oh, I have fond memories of them," she exclaimed. "I used to eat them growing up in France. They are made in the bakeries, especially in Alsace near the German border, and come in a variety of sizes. German breakfast tables are not complete without a basket of pretzels. There are small ones for the little children, medium ones for the older children and teenagers, and large ones for grandma and grandpa." She sent me a recipe, in Old German script, from a cookbook in her collection. This brioche dough must be made in a heavy-duty electric mixer and is exceptionally easy to handle. It is so delicate and delicious that it is a wonder that brioche is known as the "workhorse dough of the bakery." I use the same recipe to make Brioche Croissants, crescent breakfast rolls (page 94), in a manner similar to ones made in the Parisian bakeries.*

1.  In the workbowl of a heavy-duty mixer fitted with a paddle attachment, combine 1 cup of the flour, the yeast, sugar, and salt on low speed. Add the milk and 2 eggs and beat at medium speed for 2 minutes, or until smooth. Add the remaining 3 eggs, one at a time, beating well after each addition. Gradually beat in 2 more cups of the flour, ½ cup at a time.

2. When the flour has been incorporated, on low speed, add the butter a few pieces at a time. Beat just until completely incorporated. Reduce the speed to low and gradually add the remaining 1½ cups flour. Beat until thoroughly blended and smooth in consistency. The dough will be soft, yet it will hold its own shape. With a rubber spatula, scrape the dough into a greased bowl. Cover tightly with plastic wrap and let rise at cool room temperature until doubled in bulk, about 3 hours. Gently deflate the dough with a spatula, cover tightly, and refrigerate for 12 hours, or as long as overnight. This will give the dough time to rise slowly, firm up, and develop its wonderful flavor.

3. Remove the brioche dough from the refrigerator and let it rest at room temperature for 1 hour. Line 2 large baking sheets with parchment.

4. Turn the dough, which will still be cool, but slightly firm, out onto a lightly floured work surface. Pat the dough into a thick 14 by 14-inch square. With a chef's knife or a pastry wheel, cut the square into 12 strips of equal width. Using the palms of your hands, roll each strip back and forth with flat hands to form a 20-inch-long rope. Holding one end in each hand, bring up the two ends and cross them about 4 inches down from the tips to make a loop. Twist the loose ends together twice to make a noose. Bring the twisted end up and over the loop on the work surface, bringing it down to touch the bottom of the loop in the center. Dampen the ends of the dough with a bit of water before pressing down onto the loop to form a pretzel shape. Carefully lift off the work surface and position each pretzel on the baking sheet, about 3 inches apart. I place 6 on each baking sheet. Cover loosely with plastic wrap and let rise at cool room temperature until puffy and doubled in bulk, about 1 hour.

5. Preheat the oven to 350° 20 minutes before baking. Gently brush the surfaces of the pretzels with the egg glaze and sprinkle with the coarse sugar crystals.

6. Bake on the center rack of the oven for 20 to 24 minutes, or until golden brown. Remove from the pans with a metal spatula and transfer to racks to cool completely before eating.

# Brioche Croissants

Makes 24 crescent rolls

1 recipe Brioche Pretzel dough
(page 92), through step 3

1 egg beaten with 1 tablespoon
milk, for glaze

*Not many American bakers know that croissants, known for centuries as* panis lunatis, *or "bread of the moon," for their shape, are often made from the egg- and butter-rich brioche dough. While the French breakfast roll does not have the defined layering like a classic croissant, it will have all the flavor and charm of a simple, buttery roll, cousin to the Austrian* kipfel. *There is much less labor involved in making the dough. It's almost ridiculously simple, by baker's terms. Just be sure to make the dough a day ahead so it has time to chill overnight in the refrigerator. This method of rolling out the dough into a circle and cutting it into even pie-shaped wedges is a snap. For variety, put a dab of preserves at the base before rolling it up to make a jam croissant.*

1. Turn the dough, which will still be cool, but slightly firm, out onto a lightly floured work surface and divide into 4 equal portions. Wrap 3 of the portions in plastic wrap and set aside while you work. Place the remaining portion on a lightly floured work surface and roll it out into a 12-inch-diameter circle, like for a pie crust, about $1/8$- to $1/4$-inch thick (remember, the thinner, the more delicate the roll). Roll the dough on a diagonal and make quarter turns to achieve an even circle. Keep lifting and moving the dough to prevent sticking or tearing. If the dough springs back or is hard to roll out, let it rest for a few minutes, and then continue. With a knife or a pastry wheel, divide the dough into 6 equal pie-shaped triangles. Slash a cut about 1 inch long into the center at the base of each triangle. You will have 6 large triangles from each portion.

2. To shape the croissants, with the base of a triangle facing you, spread the slit and roll over the bottom edge to start the roll. With the fingers of one hand outstretched on the base and the other hand holding the point, tightly roll the base up toward the pointed apex, moving only one hand. You will stretch the point slightly while you hold it and press down on the dough as you roll to keep the croissant from sliding around. Place each croissant on a baking sheet with the tip underneath so it won't pop out during baking. Bend the roll into a crescent shape by curving the tapered ends toward the center, leaving only an inch or two of space between the points (they spread during baking). Repeat the process with the remaining dough. Do not crowd the croissants on the baking sheets; leave 3 to 4 inches between them. Brush the tops with some of the egg glaze. Let rise, uncovered, at room temperature, until doubled in bulk, about 40 minutes. Or do this final rise in the refrigerator overnight, with the baking sheets covered with a double layer of plastic wrap, and glaze and bake the brioche croissants in the morning.

4. Preheat the oven to 425° 20 minutes before baking.

5. When the croissants are light and springy to the touch and have just lost their chill, they are ready to bake. Brush the tops with another layer of the egg glaze. Place another baking sheet of the same dimensions under each pan with the croissants to "double pan" and protect the bottoms from burning. Bake one pan at a time, on the center or lower third position, for 10 minutes. Reduce the oven temperature to 350° and bake for 8 to 10 minutes more (18 to 20 minutes total), or until golden brown. Remove from the oven and transfer to racks to cool for at least 15 minutes before serving. These are good warm or at room temperature.

## Cinnamon Breadsticks

Makes 14 breadsticks

1 ½ to 2 cups unbleached
   all-purpose flour

1 tablespoon (1 package) active
   dry yeast or 2 ½ teaspoons
   SAF fast-acting yeast

1 tablespoon sugar

1 ½ teaspoons salt

¾ cup warm milk (105° to 115°)

2 tablespoons butter, at room
   temperature, or nut oil

CINNAMON SUGAR

¾ cup sugar

3 tablespoons vanilla powder

1 tablespoon ground cinnamon

6 tablespoons butter, melted

*We're used to savory and crunchy breadsticks, but sweet? Oh, yes. I like to make these a bit thicker and shorter—more like a baton than the petite variety you find standing on your table in an Italian restaurant. This recipe is inspired by an entry in the 1993 King Arthur Winter Bake Contest. I especially like the coating; it has Cook's vanilla powder in it, available in the supermarket spice section next to the vanilla extract. Cinnamon breadsticks are great to serve to children (adults, too, especially when they are fussy eaters), and they go wonderfully with tea or cocoa. Be prepared to eat more than just one; these are positively addictive.*

1. In the workbowl of a heavy-duty mixer fitted with a paddle attachment, combine 1 cup of the flour, yeast, sugar, and salt on low speed. Add the milk and soft butter or oil and beat for 1 minute on medium speed. Gradually beat in the remaining flour, ⅓ cup at a time, until a soft dough is formed that just clears the sides of the bowl.

2. Turn out the dough onto a lightly floured work surface and knead until smooth and pliable, about 1 minute. Add 1 tablespoon of flour at a time, as necessary, to prevent sticking. The dough will be firm, yet a bit soft, but not sticky. Place in a greased 1-quart plastic container, turn once to coat the top, and cover loosely with plastic wrap. Let rise at room temperature until doubled in bulk, about 1 hour.

3. Preheat the oven to 375°. Line 2 large baking sheets with parchment. Set 2 wire cooling racks to the side of the work surface. Turn the dough out onto a lightly floured work surface

and divide in half with a bench knife. Flatten each portion into a free-form rectangle and cut each portion into 7 equal pieces. With your palms, roll each piece into an 8- to 9-inch rope about the width of your baking sheet and 1 inch thick in diameter. Place the sticks parallel to each other and no less than 1 inch apart on the baking sheet (you might be able to fit them all on one pan). Let stand at room temperature for 10 minutes, or until slightly puffy.

4. With a natural bristle pastry brush, brush the surfaces with some cold water. Bake on the center rack of the oven for 15 to 18 minutes, or until crisp and golden brown. The breadsticks will not be soft like a roll; they will be a bit dry. Transfer to cooling racks for 15 minutes.

5. Meanwhile, reduce the oven temperature to 325°. Combine the sugar, vanilla powder, and cinnamon on a shallow plate. Brush each cooled breadstick lightly with some of the melted butter. Using your hands, roll each stick in the cinnamon sugar, coating completely. Return the sticks to the cooling rack. When all of the breadsticks have been coated, place the wire rack on the baking sheet. Return the pan to the oven and bake for 15 minutes, until crisp on the outside. If you like your breadsticks very crunchy, reduce the oven temperature to 200° and bake for 25 to 30 minutes more, or until dried out. Remove the pan from the oven and let the breadsticks cool completely. Store in an airtight container at room temperature for up to 4 days.

# Ethnic and Holiday
# Special Breads

When I was in grade school, my favorite subject was physical and cultural geography. One of my first books on the subject had wonderful color drawings depicting children who lived in different geographical areas, some of their customs, their traditional clothing, and often, some type of food they ate. I poured over that book for years, taking in every detail of the drawings, even long after I outgrew the simple text.

In my geography lessons, I kept coming across the concept of the melting pot, the gradual process of cultural blending that results in creating something more dynamic than the mere sum of its parts. I visualized a big cauldron (my conception of the United States) filled to the brim with liquid and lots of different people swimming around. As I grew older, my family moved around quite a bit. In the different areas of the United States where we lived, I met other people from different countries and cultures, making lasting friendships. That old school term gained meaning as I became an integral part of the blend. Curious by nature, I always asked a lot of questions, especially about the food new acquaintances liked, and was thrilled to be asked over to dinner. I sat at many a table, quietly listening to conversations in different languages and eating beautifully prepared meals. I even studied the cookware used for serving and the array of pots and pans used in preparation.

*Fresh Strawberry Brunch Blintzes (page 101)*

As an adult, one of the joys of my life is discovering new ideas and new foods, especially baked goods, both through my own travels and those of my friends. I now live in a community composed of a variety of nationalities. My new neighbor, Ayswaria, from the Malabar Coast of India, offered to teach me to make chapatis like her mother taught her. My catering client, Mary Anne, introduced me to her favorite cookbook, *Polish Heritage Cookery*—the Polish *Joy of Cooking*—which is filled with unusual baked goods. Another friend, Jutta, from Germany, makes a wide variety of kuchens, Europe's homestyle coffee cakes, for our afternoon visits over cups of tea. My old baking assistant and friend for decades, Piedad, and I labor over tortilla recipes. I called a local Ethiopian restaurant to find out how they make an African staple bread called *injera,* which is made from teff flour. My Hungarian relatives share recipes that have never been written down by insisting that I watch them in the kitchen so that my attempts will turn out just right. When my girlfriend, Julie, whose grandmother emigrated from Russia, told me about her blini pancakes, I was transported to a distant time and place.

Such personal exchanges are how food is not only transmitted to subsequent generations, but how it evolves, as new bakers substitute new ingredients and modern equipment in an attempt to marry the flavors of the past with the tastes and techniques of the present. Traditional home baking is a precious skill. Recipes, by nature, are meant to be shared and enjoyed, all the while offering a window into a culture's cherished traditions. Baked goods that were once local specialties are now available for food lovers the world over to enjoy and create. Here are an assortment of wonderful breakfast breads, some perhaps unfamiliar, that further explore the vast world of baking.

# Fresh Strawberry Brunch Blintzes

(Illustrated on page 98)

*One of my favorite dishes to serve guests is a platter of sweet blintzes, one of the best known of Jewish brunch foods. They are crêpelike pancakes filled with a smooth, tangy cheese center that contrasts with their crisp, buttery wrapper. In my rendition, soft, velvety ricotta and cream cheeses are blended to make the simplest of fillings. This recipe is especially well suited for entertaining, since it calls for baking all the blintzes at once instead of frying them one by one on the stovetop; but I have given instructions for both methods. Though a good bit of mystique surrounds their preparation, crêpes are surprisingly easy to handle and bake up quickly once you get the wrist action of tilting the hot pan to distribute the batter evenly. (Many bakers reserve a well-seasoned pan solely for the task.) The size of the crêpes you make depends on the size of your skillet or frying pan, since the thin batter tends to spread out to the perimeter of the pan. The standard size for crêpes varies from 6 to 9 inches in diameter.*

1. To make the wrapper batter, combine the batter ingredients in a large bowl or in the bowl of a food processor. Using a handheld immersion blender, a whisk, or a food processor fitted with the metal blade, beat until smooth. Cover and refrigerate for 30 minutes to 1 hour. Lightly grease a 6- to 7-inch seasoned crêpe pan or nonstick frying pan with cooking spray. Heat the pan over medium heat until hot. Stir the batter to avoid separation. Working quickly, remove the pan from the heat and pour in about 2 tablespoons of batter, tilting and rotating the pan to completely cover the bottom. Cook until

*(continued)*

### BUTTERMILK BLINTZ WRAPPERS

$1\frac{1}{2}$ cups unbleached all-purpose or whole wheat pastry flour

$1\frac{1}{2}$ teaspoons baking powder

$1\frac{1}{3}$ cups cultured buttermilk

$\frac{2}{3}$ cup water

4 large eggs

1 teaspoon pure vanilla extract

$\frac{1}{2}$ teaspoon salt

### STRAWBERRY SAUCE

2 pint baskets fresh strawberries, rinsed and hulled

$\frac{1}{2}$ cup strawberry preserves

2 tablespoons Grand Marnier or freshly squeezed orange juice

### CHEESE FILLING

6 ounces cream cheese

2 cups whole milk ricotta cheese

$\frac{1}{4}$ cup sugar

2 large egg yolks, or 2 tablespoons liquid egg substitute

1 teaspoon pure vanilla extract

Grated zest of 1 orange

$1\frac{1}{4}$ cups sliced fresh strawberries

4 tablespoons ($\frac{1}{2}$ stick) unsalted butter, for frying the blintzes

Cold sour cream or plain yogurt, for serving

the bottom is golden brown and the top is set, about 30 seconds; do not turn the crêpe over. Slide the crêpes, cooked side up, in a single layer onto paper towels next to each other, but not overlapping to cool. Repeat with the remaining batter. (If not filling immediately, wrap the cooled wrappers in plastic wrap and refrigerate for up to 2 days.) Makes about thirty 5-inch wrappers.

2. To make the strawberry sauce, place all of the ingredients for the sauce in a food processor fitted with the metal blade or in a blender, and process until smooth. Cover and refrigerate until serving.

3. To make the filling, in a food processor with the metal blade, combine the cheeses, sugar, egg yolk, vanilla, and orange zest until just smooth.

4. To assemble the blintzes, place 1 heaping tablespoon of the filling and 1 tablespoon of the sliced strawberries at the bottom end of the cooked side of the wrapper. Fold each side over to almost meet in the center; the filling will still be at the end. Fold the blintz up from the bottom to enclose the filling, ending with the seam side down, to make a plump rectangular packet. The uncooked side of the wrapper will be on the outside. Place on a plate or in a plastic container. Cover with plastic wrap and chill until ready to cook. (The blintzes can be made to this point and frozen in a plastic container up to one month. Place a piece of parchment between the stacked layers to prevent sticking.)

5. To fry the blintzes, melt 1 tablespoon of the butter in a large skillet over medium-high heat. Place as many blintzes as will fit in the pan, seam side down. Fry for 1 to 2 minutes on each side, until crisp and golden brown. Add a bit more butter for frying each batch. Keep cooked blintzes warm on a plate, covered in foil, in a 300° oven. If frying up frozen blintzes, do not defrost first. Serve immediately with bowls of sour cream or plain yogurt and strawberry sauce on the side.

6. To bake the blintzes rather than fry them, adjust the oven rack to the lower third position and preheat the oven to 400°. Butter a piece of parchment, place on a heavy-duty baking sheet, and put in the oven to melt the butter. Arrange the packets in a single layer, seam side down, turning once to coat the tops with butter. Bake for 15 to 20 minutes, until golden and heated through. Bake frozen blintzes without defrosting in a 350° oven for 35 to 40 minutes. Serve immediately on a dessert plate topped with strawberry sauce and accompanied by a bowl of sour cream or yogurt. Store any leftover blintzes in the refrigerator.

# Banana–Cream Cheese Blintz Casserole

*One of my catering clients asked me to make this favorite blintz casserole for a brunch party. All of the ingredients of traditional blintzes are combined in a totally different fashion to make an easy-to-prepare casserole with flair and flavor.*

1. To make the filling, use a heavy-duty electric mixer on medium speed, beat all of the ingredients until smooth and well blended. Fold in the sliced bananas. Can be refrigerated in a covered container and made the day ahead (fold the bananas in just before assembling the casserole).

2. Preheat the oven to 300° (275° if using a Pyrex or dark-finish pan).

3. To make the batter, place the flour, baking powder, and salt in a mixing bowl or in the workbowl of a food processor fitted with the metal blade. Using a handheld immersion blender, a balloon whisk, or the food processor, add the melted butter, sugar, eggs, milk, and vanilla, and beat until smooth, 1 minute.

4. Grease a 9 by 13-inch baking pan. Place the sugar and cinnamon in a small bowl and stir to mix. Pour half of the batter into the prepared baking pan. Gently place large spoonfuls of the cheese and banana filling evenly over the batter. Spread slightly with the back of the spoon, without mixing the filling into the batter. Pour the remaining batter over the top of the filling. Sprinkle with the cinnamon-sugar mixture.

5. Bake on the center rack of the oven until set, about 1 hour 15 minutes. Slice the strawberries and sprinkle with some sugar. Cover and refrigerate until serving. Serve the casserole warm, passing the bowl of cold strawberries and cold sour cream separately.

---

**Makes 8 servings**

**CHEESE FILLING**

2 cups (16 ounces) cottage cheese

1 pound cream cheese, at room temperature

2 large eggs

⅔ cup sugar

3 tablespoons freshly squeezed lemon juice

½ teaspoon pure vanilla extract

Pinch of salt

2 firm bananas, sliced

**BATTER**

1 cup unbleached all-purpose flour

1 tablespoon baking powder

Large pinch of salt

8 tablespoons (1 stick) unsalted butter, melted

½ cup sugar

2 large eggs

½ cup milk

1 teaspoon pure vanilla extract

2 tablespoons sugar

1 tablespoon ground cinnamon

3 pint baskets fresh strawberries, rinsed and hulled

2 tablespoons sugar, or to taste

1 pint (2 cups) cold sour cream, for serving, optional

# Sunflower-Walnut Pain d'Epices

*Makes one 8-inch cakebread*

½ cup medium rye flour

½ cup quick-cooking rolled oats

½ cup chopped walnuts

¼ cup raw sunflower seeds

¾ teaspoon baking powder

½ teaspoon salt

¼ teaspoon aniseed or cardamom seeds, crushed with a mortar and pestle (optional)

Pinch of ground cinnamon

Pinch of ground cloves

2 large eggs

½ cup firmly packed light brown sugar

⅓ cup firmly packed dark brown sugar

2 tablespoons honey

⅓ cup vegetable oil or canola oil

1 teaspoon pure vanilla extract

*I discovered this recipe on a box of rye flour. It has no white flour, and you would think the resulting bread would be rather unpalatable, but it's actually quite wonderful. Baked in an 8-inch-square pan, the bread is another form of* pain d'epices, *the classic French honey-and-spice bread, which contains lots of rye flour. There are as many recipes for* pain d'epices *as there are bakers, as it is a mainstay of French country baking. It is a dense, moist, chewy bread not unlike its cousin, the gingerbread. Serve it in squares, with butter and fresh fruit.*

1. Preheat the oven to 350°. Grease the sides and bottom of an 8-inch-square pan (325° if using a Pyrex or dark-finish pan).

2. In a mixing bowl, combine the rye flour, oats, walnuts, sunflower seeds, baking powder, salt, and spices.

3. In a large bowl or in the workbowl of a heavy-duty electric mixer fitted with the paddle attachment, place the eggs, light and dark brown sugars, honey, oil, and vanilla. Using a whisk or with the electric mixer on low, beat until thickened and smooth, about 2 minutes. Make a well in the center of the flour mixture and pour in the wet ingredients, stirring with a wooden spoon to make a thick, sticky batter. Scrape with a rubber spatula into the prepared pan and smooth the top.

4. Bake on the center rack of the preheated oven for 30 to 35 minutes, or until a cake tester inserted into the center comes out clean and the top is dry and springs back when lightly pressed with your finger. Remove from the oven and cool completely in the pan before cutting into portions. Store covered in plastic wrap in the refrigerator for up to 4 days.

# Welsh Soda Bread

*I make many variations of Irish soda bread, sometimes with raisins, sometimes with whole wheat, sometimes with herbs and seeds. But I was surprised when I tasted a completely plain soda bread. It was a compact round, dusted with flour, and had the large characteristic gash on the top from being marked with an X, dividing the loaf into quarters called* farls. *It made the best toast, very similar in texture to English muffins, with a crust that is addictively crunchy. While "brown" whole wheat soda bread is the national bread of Ireland, this one made with white flour hails from Northern Ireland, Scotland, and the Welsh countryside. You can double this recipe for two loaves (they keep wrapped in plastic on the counter for three or four days and freeze quite well) and/or make this with half white spelt flour.*

*Makes 1 round loaf*

2 cups unbleached all-purpose flour

2 teaspoons granulated or light brown sugar

1 teaspoon salt

1 teaspoon baking soda

$\frac{1}{2}$ teaspoon cream of tartar

Scant cup cultured buttermilk

1$\frac{1}{2}$ tablespoons butter or margarine, melted

1 tablespoon sour cream or thick plain yogurt

1. Preheat the oven to 425°. Line a baking sheet with parchment or grease an 8-inch-round metal cake pan.

2. In a medium mixing bowl, combine the flour, sugar, salt, baking soda, and cream of tartar. Stir with a wooden spoon or Danish dough whisk. Make a well in the center and add the buttermilk, melted butter, and sour cream or yogurt; stir just to moisten. The dough will clump, be very soft, but not sticky. Turn out onto a lightly floured work surface and knead gently, about 15 times, until the sticky dough just comes together into a round loaf shape. Dust the top with some flour and rub it in.

3. Place the loaf on the pan. With a small sharp knife, slash the top with an X about $\frac{1}{2}$ inch deep. Bake on the center rack of the

*(continued)*

oven for 10 minutes, reduce the oven temperature to 375°, and bake for an additional 25 to 30 minutes, or until deep golden brown, the crust is hard and crusty, and the bottom sounds hollow when tapped with a finger. Remove from the oven and cool to room temperature before slicing to give the bread time to set its texture.

## Irish Soda Bread for St. Patrick's Day ❈ *Makes 1 round loaf*

*The word* whiskey *is from the Gaelic word* usquebaugh, *or "water of life." Legend has it that St. Patrick taught the Irish the art of distilling the hearty liquor. So, pull out that bottle of Bushmill's in the back of the cabinet, reserved for the occasional Irish coffee, and put it to good use in this soda bread, a loaf for the adult palate.*

½ cup currants

3 tablespoons Irish whiskey

1 recipe Welsh Soda Bread (page 105)

1 teaspoon caraway seeds, crushed with a mortar and pestle

2 tablespoons minced candied orange peel

1. In a small bowl, toss the currants with the Irish whiskey. Let stand on the counter at temperature for 1 hour to macerate.

2. Make the Welsh Soda Bread, adding the crushed caraway with the flour in step 1, and the currants and orange peel with the buttermilk in step 2. Bake as directed for the Welsh Soda Bread.

# Whole Wheat Soda Bread

*Soda bread is the Celtic contribution to the world of bread. This loaf reminds me of my great-aunt Nellie Guyton from County Cork, beloved in my mother's family for her baking. Southern Ireland is known for its good whole-meal soda breads, with or without raisins, a practical and traditional addition to everyday meals. Once you've made this bread a few times, you will be able to whip up a loaf in less than ten minutes and have it ready to be eaten in another hour. While eggs are not often an ingredient, I find they give the bread a desirable tender bite. Allow the finished loaves to cool to room temperature to set their texture; then spread slices with butter and orange marmalade.*

1. Preheat the oven to 425°. Line a baking sheet with parchment and sprinkle with rolled oats.

2. In a large bowl, combine the whole wheat and all-purpose flours, sugar, baking powder, baking soda, cream of tartar, salt, and raisins. Stir with a wooden spoon or Danish dough whisk. Make a well in the center and add the buttermilk, melted butter, and eggs; stir just to moisten. The dough will be very soft, but not sticky. Turn out onto a lightly floured work surface and knead gently, about 15 times, until the dough comes together into a round loaf shape. Divide the dough into 2 equal portions and shape into 8-inch rounds. Dust the tops with some unbleached flour.

3. Place the loaves on the pan and roll around to coat the bottom with the oats. With a sharp knife, slash the top with an X about ½ inch deep. Bake on the center rack of the oven for 15 minutes, reduce the temperature to 375°, and bake for 20 to 25 minutes more, or until deep golden brown and the bottom sounds hollow when tapped. Let cool to room temperature before slicing.

## Makes 2 round loaves

3 tablespoons quick-cooking rolled oats

2½ cups whole wheat flour

1½ cups unbleached all-purpose flour

¼ cup turbinado (raw) sugar or light or dark brown sugar (optional)

1 tablespoon baking powder

1 teaspoon baking soda

1 teaspoon cream of tartar

1½ teaspoons salt

1 cup raisins or currants, rinsed in hot water and patted dry

1¼ cups cultured buttermilk

2 tablespoons butter or margarine, melted

2 large eggs

# Strawberry Dumplings

Makes 12 dumplings

3 pint baskets fresh strawberries, hulled and halved

¾ cup sugar

PASTRY DOUGH

2¼ cups unbleached all-purpose flour or whole wheat pastry flour

⅓ cup corn flour or all-purpose flour

1 teaspoon salt

½ teaspoon baking powder

1 cup (2 sticks) cold unsalted butter, cut into pieces

¾ to 1 cup cold sour cream

3 tablespoons cold unsalted butter, cut into 8 pieces

3 tablespoons sugar, for sprinkling

*Fruit dumplings are the quintessential comfort food. As opposed to their savory cousins, which are boiled, fruit dumplings most often consist of fruit wrapped in a pie dough pastry crust and baked in the oven until delicately browned. The most famous is the apple dumpling, which typically has a piece of whole fruit in the center. Here is a delightful fresh strawberry version. Instead of baking all the dumplings together in one baking dish, try baking them in individual Pyrex custard cups.*

1.  Place the strawberries in a large bowl and toss with the sugar. Macerate at room temperature 1 hour, or until the sugar dissolves and makes a syrup.

2.  Meanwhile, make the pastry dough. Place the all-purpose and corn flours, salt, and baking powder in the workbowl of a food processor fitted with the metal blade or in the mixing bowl of a heavy-duty electric mixer. Cut in the butter until the mixture is laced with small chunks of butter and the texture is a coarse meal. Add the sour cream and mix on low just until a soft ball is formed. Gently knead a few times by hand to smooth out the dough. Do not overmix, or the pastry will be tough. Shape the dough into 2 equal oval portions and flatten slightly to a thickness of 1 inch. Use immediately or refrigerate.

3.  On a lightly floured work surface, using a rolling pin, roll out 1 portion of the dough to a thickness of ⅛ to ¼ inch. Using a 6-inch round saucer as a guide, cut out 6 rounds, rerolling the scraps if necessary. Repeat with the second portion of dough, ending up with a total of 12 circles of dough.

4. Preheat the oven to 400°. Grease the bottom and sides of a 9 by 13-inch rectangular glass baking dish or ceramic ovenproof casserole. Strain the juice from the strawberries into a 2-cup measure and set aside.

5. To form the dumplings, place a round of dough on the palm of your hand and cup your hand to form a bowl. Fill the dough with 3 heaping tablespoons of the berries. Pull the sides of the dough up and over the filling and pinch the dough edges on top with your fingers to form a slightly opened purse, leaving a ¾-inch space on top for steam to escape. Set the dumpling in the baking dish. Repeat to fill the remaining dough rounds, placing the filled dumplings side by side in the baking dish. It is important that the sides touch each other and the dish is completely filled to prevent spreading. Place a small pat of the butter into the top of each dumpling and sprinkle the tops with the remaining sugar.

6. Bake on the center rack of the oven for 25 to 30 minutes, or until golden brown. Immediately upon removing from the oven, drizzle with half of the reserved berry syrup. Set aside on a rack to cool to room temperature in the baking dish. Serve accompanied by the remaining syrup.

¼ cup golden raisins

¼ cup dried sweet or tart cherries

¼ cup finely chopped dried apricots

¼ cup orange brandy or flavored vodka

SPONGE

1 tablespoon (1 package) active dry yeast

¼ cup warm water (100°)

1¼ cups tepid (100°) evaporated milk or evaporated goat's milk

1 cup unbleached all-purpose flour

DOUGH

3 large eggs

Grated zest of 1 orange and 1 lemon

1½ teaspoons ground cardamom

2 teaspoons salt

½ cup mild honey, such as orange or wildflower

1 cup rye flour

8 tablespoons (1 stick) unsalted butter or soy margarine, at room temperature

About 3 cups unbleached all-purpose flour

½ cup chopped blanched almonds, lightly toasted

⅓ cup (about 1½ ounces) candied ginger, finely chopped

1 tablespoon unsalted butter, melted, for brushing

Confectioners' sugar, for dusting

# Rye and Honey Fruit Bread

*Mushroom-shaped breads are a long-standing custom in old European baking. I created this recipe for a spring article in one of my favorite magazines,* Veggie Life. *The magazine's test kitchen baked the loaves in clean 2-pound canned fruit cans, making a loaf a bit smaller than I originally planned. It was a great success. Serve this bread with an assortment of cheeses such as smoked Gouda and Brie, or the fabulously decadent Pashka Sweet Cheese Spread (page 152), an icy flavored vodka, and plenty of hot coffee or tea. If you're feeling inspired, decorate the snowy top with one fresh, unsprayed flower, like a nasturtium, and a few pretty leaves.*

1. In a small bowl, combine the raisins, dried cherries, and dried apricots with the liquor. Cover and macerate at room temperature about 1 hour.

2. Meanwhile, prepare the sponge. Place the yeast, water, milk, and 1 cup all-purpose flour in a large bowl or in the workbowl of a heavy-duty electric mixer fitted with the paddle attachment. Using a whisk or with the electric mixer on medium speed, beat until smooth, about 1 minute. Cover with plastic wrap and let rest at room temperature until bubbly, about 1 hour.

3. To make the dough, add the eggs, zest, cardamom, salt, honey, and rye flour to the sponge and beat with the whisk or with the electric mixer on low speed until smooth. Add the butter, a few pieces at a time, and beat until incorporated. Add the macerated fruit and its liquor. Add the all-purpose flour, ½ cup at a time, to form a soft dough that just clears the sides of the bowl (switch to a wooden spoon when necessary if making by hand).

*(continued)*

4. Turn out the dough onto a lightly floured work surface and knead until smooth, shiny, and soft, about 2 minutes for a machine-mixed dough and 3 to 4 minutes for a hand-mixed dough. Add 1 tablespoon of flour at a time, as necessary, to prevent sticking. It is important that this dough remain very soft and pliable. Place in a greased deep bowl, turn once to coat the top, and cover loosely with plastic wrap. Let rise at room temperature until doubled in bulk, $1\frac{1}{2}$ to 2 hours.

5. Turn out the dough onto the work surface and pat into a fat 12 by 17-inch rectangle. Sprinkle with the almonds and chopped ginger. Fold the dough over and knead gently to evenly distribute. Divide the dough into 2 equal portions. Place each in a greased 7-inch charlotte mold, or make one loaf in a 2-pound coffee can or 5-pound honey tin. Cover loosely with buttered plastic wrap and let rise at room temperature until about $\frac{1}{2}$ inch above the rim of the mold, about 40 minutes. Place the oven rack on the lowest position.

6. Twenty minutes before baking, place the oven rack in the lower third position and preheat the oven to 350°. Bake until golden brown and a cake tester inserted into the center comes out clean, 35 to 40 minutes. If the tops brown too quickly, cover loosely with a piece of aluminum foil.

7. Remove the pans from the oven and immediately transfer the baked loaves from their molds to a rack. Brush the warm tops with melted butter and dust with confectioners' sugar shaken through a metal sieve. Let cool completely and serve at room temperature cut into long wedges.

# Breakfast Italian-Style: Boboli ✽ Makes one 12-inch flatbread

*Boboli is a commercially made yeasted flatbread that is baked like the puffy focaccia, the bready cousin of Italian pizza. Baked with a coating of cheese, it is widely available in an individual size and a larger 12-inch round. I keep a few Boboli around for emergency meals, since it makes a fast and toothsome breakfast spread with a soft cheese and topped with fresh fruit—which, by the way, are standard pizza toppings in Italy.*

1 (12-inch) Boboli crust (1 16-ounce crust or 2 8-ounce crusts)

8 ounces cream cheese, soy cream cheese, ricotta cheese, kefir cheese, fresh goat cheese, or mascarpone

1½ tablespoons butter, melted, or nut oil, such as walnut or macadamia nut

Fresh fruit (suggestions follow)

Raw sugar, for sprinkling (optional)

1.  Preheat the oven to 450°. Place the Boboli on an ungreased baking sheet or pizza pan and spread it with your choice of cheese, leaving a ¾-inch border all the way around. brush the edges of the dough with the melted butter. Arrange the fruit on top (see suggestions) and press into the cheese slightly.

2.  Bake on the center rack of the oven for 10 minutes, or until the edges are deep brown. The cheese may soften or get runny, but it will firm up as the Boboli cools. Cut into wedges and serve hot.

## Fruit Toppings

Peel, core, and slice 2 large pears and arrange on top in a pinwheel design. ✽ Top the Boboli with thick slices of banana. ✽ Top with sliced or halved fresh strawberries. ✽ Top with ½ pint fresh boysenberries or blackberries. ✽ Peel, seed, and slice ¼ of a cantaloupe melon and arrange on top in a pinwheel design. ✽ Pit and slice 4 fresh plums and arrange on top. ✽ Top with stemmed and halved fresh black or white figs. ✽ Peel, seed, and slice a papaya, dot with some blueberries, and arrange on top.

# Bienenstichkuchen-The Bee Sting Cake

*Makes one 9-inch cake*

## CAKE BATTER

3 cups unbleached all-purpose flour

⅔ cup warm milk (105° to 115°)

3 tablespoons sugar

1 tablespoon (1 package) active
   dry yeast

2 large eggs, at room temperature

1 teaspoon almond extract

Pinch of salt

8 tablespoons (1 stick) unsalted
   butter, at room temperature
   and cut into 16 pieces

## CUSTARD CREAM

1 (3½-ounce) package instant
   vanilla pudding

8 ounces cream cheese, at room
   temperature

## NUT CRUST GLAZE

8 tablespoons (1 stick) unsalted
   butter, at room temperature

½ cup granulated sugar

½ cup light brown sugar

2 tablespoons milk

½ cup (2 ounces) slivered blanched
   almonds or chopped walnuts

*This country-style layer cake made from a yeast batter has been traditionally served as a rustic wedding cake. It is called a bee sting cake because of the crackly carmelized nut glaze on its dome-like top that resembles an old-fashioned conical straw beehive. While some versions call for a homemade, cheese-rich custard, this one, from a good German baker's grandmother, uses convenient modern-day packaged vanilla pudding with delicious results. This type of home-baked yeast torten is very popular throughout central Europe as a brunch coffee cake. For large parties, double the recipe and bake in an 11 by 17-inch baking sheet, then cut it into squares (you can leave out the custard filling).*

1.  Place the flour in a large bowl or in the workbowl of a heavy-duty electric mixer fitted with a paddle attachment. Make a well in the center of the flour and pour in half of the milk. Sprinkle with a tablespoon of the sugar and the yeast. Sprinkle a bit of the flour over the yeast and let stand until foamy, about 15 minutes.

2.  Add the remaining milk, remaining sugar, eggs, almond extract, and salt. Using a whisk or with the electric mixer on medium speed, beat until creamy, about 30 seconds. Add the butter pieces and beat until a smooth dough is formed, 1 to 2 minutes. If making by hand, turn the dough out of the bowl onto a lightly floured work surface and knead for 3 minutes, keeping the dough as soft as possible; if making in a mixer, knead with a dough hook for 1 minute, and then scrape down the sides of the mixing bowl. Place the dough ball back in the

bowl and grease the sides and top of the dough. Cover loosely with plastic wrap and let rise at room temperature until doubled in bulk, about 1½ hours.

3. While the dough is rising, prepare the filling. To make the filling, prepare the vanilla pudding according to package directions. Let cool just until warm. Using an electric mixer fitted with the paddle attachment, combine the vanilla pudding and the cream cheese. Beat on medium speed until smooth. Scrape into a small bowl. Place plastic wrap directly on the surface of the custard and refrigerate for at least 3 hours before filling the cake. The filling can be made the day ahead, if desired.

4. Preheat the oven to 350°. Cut out a piece of parchment to fit a 9-inch springform pan. Grease the parchment and set in the pan. Scrape the dough into the pan and press to smooth out the surface. Cover loosely with plastic wrap and let rest for 30 minutes.

5. To make the glaze, melt the butter in a medium skillet over moderate heat. Add the white and brown sugars and milk; bring to a boil, stirring constantly, and boil for 30 seconds to dissolve the sugar; the mixture will be soft and spreadable. Remove from the heat and stir in the nuts. Let cool until just warm, about 10 minutes.

6. With a small metal spatula, gently spread the warm glaze evenly over the surface of the dough. Place the oven rack in the lower third position. Bake for 35 to 40 minutes, or until golden brown and a cake tester inserted into the center comes out clean. The nuts will be golden. The topping will be a baked-on glaze. Place the cake on a wire rack and remove the spring sides. Cool completely, and then slide the cake off the bottom pan onto the rack.

7. Using a long, serrated knife, cut the cake in half horizontally. Place the bottom layer, cut side up, on a cake plate and spread evenly with all of the chilled filling. Spread the filling right up to the edges. Cover with the top layer, cut side down. Refrigerate until ready to serve.

¼ cup warm water (105° to 115°)

1½ tablespoons (1½ packages)
    active dry yeast

Pinch of sugar

1 cup warm milk (105° to 115°)

½ cup walnut oil

1 large egg plus 2 egg yolks

½ cup sugar

2 teaspoons pure vanilla extract

1 teaspoon salt

Grated zest of 1 orange

½ cup potato starch flour

3½ to 4 cups unbleached
    all-purpose flour

8 tablespoons (1 stick) unsalted
    butter, at room temperature
    and cut into pieces

8 perfect walnut halves,
    for decorating

**SWEET WALNUT FILLING**

5 ounces (1¼ cups) walnut meats

1½ tablespoons ground cinnamon

3½ cups miniature marshmallows
    or chopped regular-sized marsh-
    mallows

1¼ cups dried tart cherries or
    golden raisins or a mixture
    of the two

# Walnut Babka

*If you are not Polish or Jewish, you're probably not familiar with this sweet, egg-raised pastry that is the culinary trademark of Old Polish baking. A bridge between peasant hospitality and gourmet fare,* babka *can vary from a chocolate marble version to one stuffed with fresh plums or dried fruit. The marshmallow filling and layering technique, created by baker Marcy Goldman, is a fast substitution for the traditional method of making a meringue to suspend the sweet filling ingredients.* Babka *dough is similar to the Hungarian* beigli, *only it is baked in a tube mold that is wider at the top than bottom (these pans are not available in the United States, so I substitute a Bundt pan).* Babka *is best served, toasted, for a brunch dessert rather than for early morning breakfast (a Polish breakfast typically consists of rolls with farmer's cheese and chives, cold cuts, or eggs). If you like chocolate, add 2 tablespoons of unsweetened cocoa with the walnuts and cinnamon.*

1. Place the warm water in a small bowl. Sprinkle the yeast and pinch of sugar over the water and stir to dissolve. Let the mixture stand until foamy, about 10 minutes.

2. In the workbowl of a heavy-duty electric mixer fitted with a paddle attachment, combine the milk, yeast mixture, walnut oil, eggs, sugar, vanilla, salt, zest, potato starch flour, and 2 cups of flour and mix on low speed. Beat until a smooth batter is formed, about 2 minutes. Add the butter, waiting for the pieces to be incorporated before adding more. Switch to the dough hook. Add the remaining flour, ½ cup at a time, to form a soft dough that just clears the sides of the bowl. Let the machine knead the dough for 2 minutes.

3. Turn the dough out onto a lightly floured work surface and knead gently until a very soft, springy dough ball is formed, about 30 seconds. Add 1 tablespoon of flour at a time, as necessary, to prevent sticking. (This dough is very rich and does not require a long kneading time, as it can easily absorb too much flour.) Place in a greased deep container, turn once to coat the top, and cover loosely with plastic wrap. Let rise at room temperature until doubled in bulk, about 1½ hours.

4. Meanwhile, prepare the filling: Place the walnuts and cinnamon in the bowl of a food processor fitted with the metal blade, and grind. Set aside. Put the cherries or raisins in a small bowl with hot water to cover, and let stand to plump, at least 30 minutes.

5. Grease a 12-cup (standard) fluted Bundt pan with melted butter or spray with butter-flavored vegetable cooking spray. Arrange the walnut halves around the bottom of the pan, flat side up. Drain the dried fruit and pat dry with paper towels. Turn the dough out onto the work surface. Divide the dough into 3 equal portions and roll each into a 10 by 12-inch rectangle. Distribute one-third of the marshmallows over the dough, and then sprinkle with one-third of the ground walnuts and one-third of the dried fruit. Beginning at the long edge, roll up tightly in jelly roll fashion, leaving the ends open. Set aside and repeat with the remaining 2 portions of dough.

6. Lay a log of dough into the bottom of the prepared pan over the walnut halves and wrap it completely around the center tube. Layer the remaining 2 logs of filled dough on top of it, staggering the open ends. Don't worry about any particular design; the dough will all rise together, forming a swirl effect. Cover loosely with plastic and set aside at room temperature to rise for 1 to 1½ hours, or until the dough comes to 1 inch above the rim of the pan. You can also cover the pan with a double layer of greased plastic wrap and let it rise in the refrigerator overnight; then bake in the morning to have the babka fresh for a late breakfast or brunch.

7. Preheat the oven to 350° 20 minutes before baking. (If your babka has risen overnight in the refrigerator, let it stand at room temperature while the oven preheats.)

8. Bake on the center rack of the oven for 55 to 65 minutes, or until golden brown and a cake tester inserted in the center comes out clean. Remove from the oven and let cool in the pan for 10 minutes before inverting onto a wire rack. Let cool for at least 1 hour before slicing. Store in the refrigerator.

# Entertaining for Breakfast: All Types of Coffee Cakes

I want you, the baker, to have a wide range of delicious coffee cakes from which to choose. There are baking powder coffee cakes, including crumb cakes and plain butter cakes, and my "in-a-pinch" coffee cakes, made from a cake mix (our secret, please!). The latter are meant to be faster to prepare than the ones in the same genre made with yeast, a leavener very popular in European pastry. Each just-baked classic in this collection is a favorite, some a bit more decadent than others, all contemporary, luscious, and appealing. They come in a range of sweetnesses, but all share one thing in common—they are meant to be eaten alongside a hot cup of something.

Simple, unadorned coffee cakes can be plain, gently spiced, or boast an added layer of fruit. They are not frosted, but often have a layer or topping of crumbs, called streusel, and can be made in a round or rectangular single layer, to be eaten right out of the pan, or baked in deep tube pans, with the cake taking the shape of the pan. In such a cake, the hollow tube center allows the oven heat to be evenly distributed to the middle of the cake during baking. I use a Bundt pan or fluted tube molds, which look nice on a table. The main ingredient is usually butter, which gives a tender crumb, but I have used different types of oils—nut, olive, and vegetable—with success, though the flavor will vary dramatically depending on the combination of ingredients. I have

*Vanilla and Cinnamon Crumb Cake (page 122)*

made sure to include a quintessential crumb cake and a sour cream tube cake, both of which are substantial and special at the same time.

A coffee cake is usually very moist, and quite fragile, coming directly out of the oven because the base is a tender cake. As it cools on a cake rack, however, its crumb will contract and settle, making it easy to slice. To unmold a tube cake, place a wire cake rack over the top rim of the cake pan. Place your outstretched palm against the rack to secure it and gently flip the pan upside down onto the rack. The cake will release onto the rack. If you are using a springform pan, you just pop off the sides and serve the cake off the bottom of the pan.

Coffee cakes are really best a few hours out of the oven, but they are nice to have in the freezer "just in case." They can be served as a conclusion to a meal early in the day, or stand on their own with coffee.

# Apple Pie Coffee Cake

*In colonial America, apple pie was served with breakfast or with lunch as a side dish. This was the first coffee cake I ever made. I got the recipe when I was eighteen years old on a summer visit to my Aunt Joan, who then lived in North Carolina. I loved the intense apple flavor and the cinnamon-brown-colored batter cooked all around it. It is so homey, you'd be hard-pressed to find the recipe in any cookbook.*

1. Preheat the oven to 375° (350° if using a Pyrex or dark-finish pie plate). Grease a 10-inch pie plate.

2. In a medium bowl, combine the eggs, oil, vanilla, and sugar, beating with a wooden spoon until thick, about 1 minute. Add the flour, baking powder, cinnamon, allspice or nutmeg, and salt. Beat vigorously until the batter has a crumbly consistency, about 1 minute. Fold in the apples and mix until the apples are evenly coated and the batter becomes moist and smooth. There will be lots of apples, held together by a relatively stiff batter.

3. Scrape the batter into the prepared pan and smooth into an even layer with a metal spatula. Sprinkle the top evenly with the sugar. Bake on the center rack of the oven 30 to 35 minutes, until the center is firm when gently pressed. A cake tester inserted into the center should come out clean, the top and the bottom of the cake should be deep brown, and the apples should be tender when pierced with a knife. Remove from the oven and cool at least 1 hour in the pan on a folded tea towel. Serve warm or room temperature, cut in wedges from the pie pan.

*Makes one 10-inch coffee cake*

2 large eggs

1 tablespoon vegetable oil

$\frac{1}{4}$ teaspoon pure vanilla extract

$\frac{3}{4}$ cup sugar

1 cup unbleached all-purpose white flour

2 teaspoons baking powder

$\frac{1}{2}$ teaspoon ground cinnamon

$\frac{1}{4}$ teaspoon ground allspice or nutmeg

$\frac{1}{4}$ teaspoon salt

2 cups peeled, cored, and thinly sliced firm tart apples (about $1\frac{1}{2}$ pounds)

1 tablespoon turbinando (raw) sugar, for sprinkling on top

# Vanilla and Cinnamon Crumb Cake

(Illustrated on page 118)

(Illustrated on page 118)

*Makes one 10-inch round coffee cake*

## CRUMB TOP

1½ cups cake flour

⅔ cup sugar

1½ teaspoons ground cinnamon

1 teaspoon pure vanilla extract

10 tablespoons (1 stick plus 2 table-spoons) cold unsalted butter, cut into small pieces

## CAKE BATTER

6 tablespoons (¾ stick) unsalted butter, at room temperature

¾ cup sugar

3 large eggs

2 teaspoons pure vanilla extract

2¼ cups cake flour, unsifted

1½ teaspoons ground cinnamon

1 teaspoon baking powder

1 teaspoon baking soda

¼ teaspoon salt

1 cup sour cream (not fat-reduced)

*This is a sublime basic coffee cake. It has a soft, deep spice-cake layer under a crust of sweet crumb. Use cake flour for the most delicate texture, but all-purpose flour will do in a pinch. I especially like baking with the premium China Tunghing cassia cinnamon and pure bourbon vanilla extract from Penzeys Spices for their strong, sweet flavors. This cake is best served the day it is baked, but it may be frozen, wrapped tightly in plastic wrap and then aluminum foil, for up to one month. Defrost it in its wrappings before reheating.*

1. Preheat the oven to 350° (325° for a dark-finish pan). Line a 10-inch springform pan with parchment, grease the bottom and sides and set aside.

2. To make the crumb top, in the bowl of a heavy-duty electric mixer fitted with the paddle attachment, combine the flour, sugar, and cinnamon. Cut in the vanilla and cold butter on low speed until coarse dry crumbs are formed. Pour into a small bowl and set aside. If not using immediately, refrigerate until needed.

3. To make the cake batter, without cleaning the mixing bowl, cream the butter and sugar on medium speed until light and fluffy, about 1 minute. Add the eggs, one at a time, and the vanilla extract and beat well on medium speed for 30 seconds. The mixture will be loose. Add the flour, cinnamon, baking powder, baking soda, and salt and beat on low speed for 15 seconds. Add the sour cream and beat on medium-high speed only until the lumps smooth out and the mixture looks fluffy, about 30 seconds on medium-high speed. Do not overbeat.

4. Spread the batter evenly into the prepared springform pan. Sprinkle the top evenly with the crumb topping. Bake on the center rack of the oven for 45 to 55 minutes, or until the top is crisp and feels firm when gently touched in the center, the cake separates slightly from the sides of the pan, and a cake tester inserted into the center comes out clean (it may be a bit moist; that's okay). Do not overbake, or the cake will be dry. Remove from the oven and cool in the pan on a wire rack for 5 minutes before removing the sides of the pan. Let cool at least 30 minutes before serving warm, or cover in plastic wrap to serve later at room temperature. Store at room temperature for up to 3 days.

# Fresh Pineapple Upside-Down Cake

Makes one 9-inch cake

## TOPPING

4 tablespoons (½ stick) unsalted butter, melted

½ cup firmly packed light brown sugar

¼ cup firmly packed dark brown sugar

5 slices (½ inch thick) fresh pineapple rings (about 1 pineapple)

8 dried or fresh apricot halves, whole canned or fresh pitted sweet cherries, or ½-inch-thick pieces of fresh papaya

## CAKE

8 tablespoons (1 stick) unsalted butter, at room temperature

¾ cup granulated sugar

2 large eggs

1¼ teaspoons pure vanilla extract

¾ cup unbleached all-purpose flour

¾ cup cake flour

2 teaspoons baking powder

½ teaspoon ground cinnamon

¼ teaspoon salt

½ cup milk

*Pineapple upside-down cake was the home culinary craze after the Dole Company of Hawaii ran a cooking contest in 1925 asking for recipes featuring their canned pineapple, developed in 1903. This is the real thing, made all the better by using fresh instead of canned pineapple. The fruit and sugar caramelizes while the cake bakes, so when the cake is inverted after baking, the bottom layer becomes a glazed-fruit topping. I was given this recipe by a friend who worked as a waitress in the café at Chez Panisse restaurant in Berkeley, California. As I've made it over the years, the recipe has evolved, and I adjust the ingredients and proportions ever so slightly each time. In the spirit of California cuisine, the pineapple is accented with some apricots, cherries, papaya chunks, or even banana slices, making each cake just a little bit different.*

1. Preheat the oven to 350°. Grease the bottom and sides of a 9 by 2-inch round metal cake pan.

2. To make the topping, in a small bowl, with a rubber spatula, stir together the melted butter and brown sugars. Spread the mixture in the prepared pan. Drain the pineapple on a double layer of paper towels and then transfer it to the pan, arranging it decoratively in one layer on top of the sugar. I put a whole ring in the center and arrange half rings around it. Set an apricot half, a cherry, or a piece of papaya in the curve of each ring. It is okay that there is some space between the fruit. Set aside.

3. To make the coffee cake, in the workbowl of a heavy-duty electric mixer, cream the butter and sugar on low speed until light and fluffy, about 1 minute. Add the eggs and vanilla extract, and beat until smooth. In another bowl, combine the all-purpose and cake flours, baking powder, cinnamon, and salt on low speed. Add the dry mixture to the creamed mixture alternately with the milk, beating well after each addition. Beat hard until the batter has a creamy consistency, about 1 minute.

4. Scrape the batter into the prepared pan over the pineapple. Bake on the center rack of the oven for 45 to 50 minutes, or until a cake tester inserted into the center comes out clean. Remove from the oven and let stand on a rack for 5 to 8 minutes. Run a knife around the edge and place a plate on top. Invert the cake carefully onto the plate; it should come out easily. Serve warm or at room temperature.

# Blueberry Buckle

Makes one 9 by 13-inch coffee cake

### CRUMB FILLING

16 amaretti cookies (about 4 ounces)

¾ cup firmly packed light brown sugar

1½ teaspoons ground cinnamon

### CAKE BATTER

8 tablespoons (1 stick) unsalted butter, at room temperature

1 cup sugar

3 large eggs

1 teaspoon pure vanilla extract

1 teaspoon almond extract

1 cup sour cream (not fat-reduced)

2 cups unbleached all-purpose flour

1 teaspoon baking soda

½ teaspoon salt

### FRUIT TOPPING

3 cups fresh blueberries, rinsed, dried, and picked over

2 tablespoons unbleached all-purpose flour

Confectioners' sugar, for dusting

*You don't see coffee cake–style buckles much these days. They belong in the family of cobblers and shortcakes, which combine fresh fruit, dough, and a littering of spiced crumbs. Buckles come to us from the days when all baked goods were made at home, often with few ingredients. They are a homemade pleasure from rural America, always made with berries and a tender egg yolk–rich yellow cake. After baking, this buckle is cut into squares, ending up quite like a square muffin. (It is supposed to "buckle" in the middle from so many berries, but never quite seems to.) You can use one type of berry, as I do here, or a combination of blueberries and raspberries or blackberries.*

1. Preheat the oven to 350° (325° for a Pyrex or dark-finish pan). Grease the bottom and sides of a 9 by 13-inch baking pan. Set aside.

2. To make the filling, place the amaretti in a small bowl and, using your thumb, coarsely crush the cookies. Combine with the brown sugar and cinnamon. Set aside.

3. Using a heavy-duty electric mixer on medium speed, cream the butter and sugar until light and fluffy, about 1 minute. Add the eggs, one at a time, the vanilla and almond extracts, and the sour cream; beat well on medium-low speed for 30 seconds. Add the flour, baking soda, and salt, and beat for about 30 seconds on medium-high speed, until thick and fluffy. Do not overbeat.

4. Spread half of the batter evenly into the prepared pan. Sprinkle all but 2 tablespoons of the crumb filling over the surface. Top

with the remaining batter, smoothing the top. In a large bowl, toss the berries with the flour and distribute evenly over the top of the batter. Sprinkle with the remaining crumbs.

5. Bake on the center rack of the oven for 50 to 60 minutes, or until a cake tester inserted into the center comes out clean. Remove from the oven and cool in the pan on a wire rack at least 20 minutes before cutting. Sprinkle with confectioners' sugar pressed through a sieve with the back of a spoon, or sifted. Serve warm, cut into 12 squares, or cover with plastic to serve later at room temperature.

# Fresh Fruit Kuchen

*not very good*

2 pounds Italian purple plums or fresh apricots, halved and pitted, or 3½ pounds very ripe, but firm and good-flavored fresh peaches

1 cup unbleached all-purpose flour

1 cup cake flour

½ cup granulated sugar

2½ teaspoons baking powder

½ teaspoon salt

1 cup milk

1 large egg

½ cup vegetable or canola oil

1 teaspoon pure vanilla extract

3 tablespoons granulated or turbinando (raw) sugar

½ teaspoon ground cinnamon

¼ teaspoon ground nutmeg or mace

3 tablespoons freshly squeezed lemon juice

½ cup confectioners' sugar, for dusting

*This recipe, given to me by my friend Connie Rothermal, has a simple, unassuming name, almost deceptively so for a delectable coffee cake with such a rich history. When I started baking, my favorite coffee cake was the Peach Cake Cockaigne in the* Joy of Cooking. *I could never get over the* Cockaigne *in the title; at the time, I thought it some area in France since the Rombauers used it in quite a few recipe headings. It turns out, however, that Cockaigne is an imaginary land of plenty, a place of luxury, ease, and, obviously, many culinary delights. My homage to Cockaigne mimics, in both ingredients and method, a classic kuchen, a style of coffee cake you would be likely to find made in homes in Germany, Austria, Hungary, and the former Czechoslovakia. While the classic kuchen is made with Italian purple plum halves that end up sinking into the batter, you can use other fruits such as peaches, and combinations of fruits such as chunks or slices of apples and whole grapes, or apricots and canned or fresh cherries, which make the kuchen especially beautiful to behold.*

1. Preheat the oven to 350°. Grease the sides and bottom of a 15½ by 10½-inch jelly roll pan (it must have the 1-inch sides). I have also used a ceramic roasting pan of the same dimensions.

2. If you are using plums or apricots, they won't have to be peeled. If you use peaches, blanch them in a large saucepan of boiling water for 10 to 15 seconds. With a slotted spoon, transfer the peaches to a bowl of ice water. Place each peach on a layer of paper towel and slip off the skin with your fingers or

a paring knife. Halve and pit the peaches and cut into thick slices into a large bowl. You will have about 7 cups of fruit. *5 cups is ~~plenty~~ plenty peaches*

3. In a mixing bowl with a large whisk, combine the all-purpose and cake flours, sugar, baking powder, and salt. Make a well in the center and add the milk, egg, oil, and vanilla. Beat hard with a whisk until the batter has a stiff, smooth consistency, about 30 seconds.

4. Using a large rubber spatula, scrape the batter onto the prepared pan. With floured fingers, press the batter into the pan in an even layer. Arrange the fruit pieces in neat, even rows across and down the batter, as close together as possible, to completely cover the batter, but leaving a 1-inch rim of exposed batter around the edges. If you use two kinds of fruit, alternate the rows. If you use three, alternate sections of fruit. Combine the sugar, cinnamon, and nutmeg in a small bowl and sprinkle evenly over the fruit. Drizzle with the lemon juice by spoonfuls. Lay a piece of parchment paper loosely over the top, securing the four corners with wooden toothpicks if necessary (this helps cook the fruit more thoroughly rather than having it brown).

*I had to add extra + 5 cup flour to get right consistency.*

5. Bake on the center rack of the oven for 30 to 35 minutes, or until the sides of the cake are golden brown, a cake tester inserted into the side and center comes out clean, and the fruit is cooked and bubbly. Remove the pan from the oven, place on a rack, remove the parchment paper, and cool for at least 15 minutes before serving. Serve in squares cut from the pan, warm or at room temperature, dusted with the confectioners' sugar.

**SPICED NUT CRUMB TOPPING**

¼ cup light or dark brown sugar

¼ cup granulated sugar

½ cup unbleached all-purpose flour

1¼ teaspoons ground cinnamon

¼ teaspoon ground allspice

6 tablespoons cold unsalted butter, cut into pieces

½ cup chopped walnuts

**COFFEE CAKE**

8 tablespoons (1 stick) unsalted butter, at room temperature

½ cup light or dark brown sugar

½ cup granulated sugar

2 large eggs

1½ teaspoons pure vanilla extract

2 cups unbleached all-purpose flour

1 teaspoon baking powder

1 teaspoon baking soda

½ teaspoon apple pie spice mixture (see page 16) or ground cinnamon

¼ teaspoon salt

1 cup cultured buttermilk

½ pound fresh or frozen rhubarb, finely chopped to make 2 cups

# Rhubarb Coffee Cake

*An invitation to brunch holds with it the promise that there will be something sweet to accompany the hot cups of coffee— a role most often played by sweet, satisfying coffee cakes. Coffee cakes are the perfect vehicles for fresh seasonal fruit, but rhubarb is often overlooked, even by veteran bakers, when it comes time to prepare the shopping list. I think you will find that rhubarb makes a splendid addition to this, one of my favorite coffee cakes. For special occasions, serve the cake with a small pool of strawberry coulis on the side.*

1. Preheat the oven to 350°. Line the bottom of an 10-inch spring-form pan with parchment paper and grease the sides.

2. To make the crumb topping, combine the brown and white sugars, flour, cinnamon, and allspice in a small bowl or in the bowl of a food processor fitted with the metal blade. Cut in the butter with your fingers, or process just until the mixture forms coarse crumbs. Add the walnuts and set aside.

3. To make the coffee cake, in the workbowl of a heavy-duty electric mixer, cream the butter and sugars on low speed until light and fluffy, about 1 minute. Add the eggs and vanilla extract and beat until smooth. In another bowl, combine the flour, baking powder, baking soda, apple pie spice, and salt. Add to the creamed mixture alternately with the buttermilk. Beat on medium-high speed until the batter has a creamy consistency, about 1 minute. Stir in the rhubarb.

4. Using a rubber spatula, scrape the batter into the prepared pan. Sprinkle evenly with the crumb topping. Bake on the center rack of the oven for about 40 to 45 minutes, or until a cake tester inserted into the center comes out clean. Remove from the oven and cool in the pan on a rack. To serve, remove the sides of the springform pan, and cut into wedges.

## Strawberry Coulis ❊ Makes 2½ cups

*A coulis (pronounced koo-LEE), is a French term for a thick fruit purée that is used as a sauce. I think you will like the secret ingredient here—vanilla extract.*

> 2 pint baskets fresh whole strawberries, washed and hulled,
>   or 3 cups frozen unsweetened strawberries
>
> 3 tablespoons freshly squeezed lemon juice
>
> 2 tablespoons sugar or to taste
>
> 1 teaspoon pure vanilla extract

Place the berries in a large bowl and sprinkle with the lemon juice and sugar. Let stand at least 1 hour to macerate. If the berries are frozen, just let them sit until they defrost. Place the fruit in a food processor fitted with the metal blade, add the vanilla, and process until smooth. Pour into a storage container or a glass pitcher with a lid. Store in the refrigerator until serving. Serve chilled.

# Old-Fashioned Sour Cream Coffee Cake

**NUT CRUMB**

⅓ cup light brown sugar

⅓ cup granulated sugar

2 teaspoons ground cinnamon

½ teaspoon ground nutmeg
  or mace

1 cup pecans


4 cups unbleached all-purpose flour

4 teaspoons baking powder

1 teaspoon baking soda

½ teaspoon ground nutmeg
  or mace

1 teaspoon salt

1 cup (2 sticks) unsalted butter,
  at room temperature

2⅓ cups granulated sugar

4 large eggs

1 tablespoon pure vanilla extract

½ teaspoon almond extract

2 cups sour cream

¼ cup cultured buttermilk


¾ cup chopped pitted dates

3 tablespoons confectioners' sugar,
  for dusting

*I serve this cake (which has to be the richest version ever of the famous Jewish culinary classic) with fresh jumbo strawberries for brunch. A fluted pan with a 12-cup capacity, known as a Bundt pan, will bake the batter into a large, handsome cake that is suitable for a pedestal cake stand; an angel food cake pan will work as well. I like to bake this cake in the star Bundt pan, which was created by Nordic Ware in honor of the fiftieth anniversary of their creation of the original Bundt pan in 1949.*

1.  Preheat the oven to 350° (325° if using a dark-finish pan). Grease and flour a 10-inch plain or fluted tube pan, 12-cup (standard) Bundt pan, or two 9 by 5-inch loaf pans and set aside.

2.  To make the nut crumbs, place all of the ingredients for the nut crumb in a food processor fitted with the metal blade, and pulse until the nuts are finely chopped. Set aside.

3.  To make the cake, in a medium bowl, combine the flour, baking powder, baking soda, nutmeg, and salt. Set aside.

4.  In the large workbowl of a heavy-duty electric mixer, cream the butter and sugar on medium speed until light and fluffy, about 1 minute. Add the eggs, one at a time, beating thoroughly after each addition. Add the vanilla and almond extracts, sour cream, and buttermilk, blending on medium-high speed just until smooth.

5. With the electric mixer on low speed, gradually add the dry ingredients to the sour cream mixture. After all of the dry ingredients have been added, beat well on medium speed until fluffy and smooth yet thick, about 2 minutes. There should be no lumps or dry spots.

6. With a large rubber spatula, scrape half of the batter into the prepared tube pan. Sprinkle with half of the nut crumb mixture and distribute the dates around the mold; top with the rest of the batter. Sprinkle with the remaining nut crumb. Use a small metal spatula or flat knife to smooth the top layer, making sure no filling is showing.

7. Bake on the center rack of the oven for 60 to 70 minutes, or until a cake tester comes out clean and the top of the cake is no longer shiny. Remove from the oven and let stand in the pan for 20 minutes. Remove from the pan by carefully inverting the cake onto a rack to cool completely. Place the rack over a piece of waxed paper, and dust the cake with the confectioners' sugar. Transfer the cooled cake to a serving plate. Serve at room temperature, cut into wedges. This cake freezes well for up to 2 months; dust with confectioners' sugar just before serving.

# Black, White, and Mocha Coffee Cake

Makes one 10-inch cake

8 ounces semisweet or bittersweet
  chocolate, broken into pieces

1¼ tablespoons instant espresso
  powder

3 cups unbleached all-purpose flour

1½ teaspoons baking powder

1½ teaspoons baking soda

¼ teaspoon salt

8 tablespoons (1 stick) unsalted
  butter, at room temperature

1½ cups sugar

4 large eggs

1 tablespoon pure vanilla extract

2 cups sour cream

Whole fresh strawberries,
  for serving

*This superb variation on a plain sour cream coffee cake is destined to change your culinary life. It is so luscious and pretty that I consider it one of the best cakes I make. The recipe came to me from former* Food & Wine *magazine editor Susan Wyler. I wish I could say that I improved upon it, but it is perfect just as she created it (although I did add a touch of coffee). Don't be intimidated by the two different colored batters and swirling them—it's a snap.*

1.  Preheat the oven to 325° (300° if using a dark-finish pan). Grease and flour a 10-inch plain or fluted tube or Bundt pan and set aside.

2.  In the top of a double boiler, melt the chocolate and espresso powder over hot water, stirring until smooth. Remove from the heat and set aside. In a medium bowl, combine the flour, baking powder, baking soda, and salt. Set aside.

3.  In a large workbowl of a heavy-duty electric mixer, cream the butter and sugar on medium speed until light and fluffy, about 1 minute. Add the eggs, one at a time, beating thoroughly after each addition. Add the vanilla and sour cream, blending on low speed just until smooth; the batter will be very thick. Beat an additional 30 seconds on high speed.

4.  Gradually add the dry ingredients to the sour cream mixture and beat on low speed until fluffy and smooth yet thick, 1 to 2 minutes. There should be no lumps or dry spots. Remove 1 cup of the batter, place in a small bowl, and stir in the melted chocolate.

5. With a large spatula, scrape half of the vanilla batter into the prepared pan. Gently top with half of the chocolate batter. Layer the remaining vanilla batter over the top and finish with the remaining chocolate batter. Place a butter knife straight down into the batter and gently swirl around the pan once or twice, marbling the batters.

6. Bake on the center rack of the oven for 60 to 65 minutes, or until a cake tester inserted into the center of the cake comes out clean and the top of the cake is no longer shiny. Remove from the pan and let stand in the pan for 15 minutes. Remove from the pan by inverting the cake onto a rack; cool completely. Serve with the center tube filled with whole fresh berries.

# Fast Coffee Cakes: When Time Is of the Essence

Do I ever reach for a boxed cake mix? Indeed I do, and with great pleasure. Matter of fact, they were the first type of cake I made when learning to bake as a teenager in the '60s. Recipes using commercial cake mixes as a main ingredient became very popular in the '70s and '80s. Sometimes I need an old-fashioned tube coffee cake recipe for a spur-of-the-moment occasion—one that is mixed, assembled, and baked in the shortest time possible. But at the same time, I want something that tastes special, something moist-textured and visually beautiful that I can serve with pride.

I have made the following three recipes dozens of times each—for brunches, as well as for buffets and birthday gifts. No one has ever been able to tell they were made with a mix, as they are not overly sweet, so be prepared for the surprised look when your guests read the recipes they request. Take care not to underbeat the batters and never mix more than one batch at a time; for some reason they don't rise properly if you make two batters at once. Use the plain mixes, not the ones with the pudding already added. The cakes are very delicate, so be sure not to open the oven door during baking. Let them cool a while after removing them from the oven to firm them up, or they will break apart.

The pecan coffee cake was given to me by my old friend Marcie Ralston Ansel, who learned it while baking for the now defunct Perfect Recipe restaurant in Palo Alto's Stanford Shopping Center twenty years ago. The Mexican double chocolate cake is so rich and decadent, you may not want anyone to know it's your "in a pinch" secret. The cornmeal cake is a sweet and featherlight cake. It makes what I call my "deep-dish" cornbread because it rises high and is so delicate that you won't need butter. Each cake yields fifteen to twenty slices and freezes perfectly.

# Pecan Sour Cream Coffee Cake

1. Grease and flour a 10-inch angel food cake tube pan; set aside. Preheat the oven to 325°.

2. To make the filling, place the pecans, brown sugar, and cinnamon in the bowl of a food processor fitted with the metal blade. Process to finely chop the nuts. Set aside.

3. To make the cake, in a large workbowl of a heavy-duty electric mixer, combine the cake mix, pudding mix, sour cream, water, oil, butter, and eggs on low speed, adding the ingredients one at a time. Beat on medium-high speed for 3 minutes, scraping the bowl often. The batter will be smooth and creamy.

4. Pour one-third of the batter into the prepared pan. Sprinkle evenly with half of the nut mixture. Pour in another third of the batter and sprinkle with the remaining nut mixture to make 2 layers of filling. Top with remaining batter. Bake on the center rack of the oven for 60 to 65 minutes, or until a cake tester inserted into the center comes out clean and the cake springs back when touched lightly. Remove from the oven and cool on a wire rack about 1 hour before turning out of the pan.

*Makes one 10-inch tube cake*

**SPICED NUT FILLING**

1 cup pecans

2/3 cup firmly packed light brown sugar

1 tablespoon ground cinnamon

1 (18¼-ounce) package yellow cake mix (such as Duncan Hines Deluxe Yellow Cake)

1 (3½-ounce) package instant vanilla pudding mix

1 cup sour cream

½ cup hot water

¼ cup vegetable oil

2 tablespoons unsalted butter, melted

4 large eggs

# Mexican Chocolate Cake

*Makes one 10-inch tube cake*

1 (18¼-ounce) package devil's food
cake mix (such as Duncan Hines
Deluxe Devil's Food Cake)

1 (3½-ounce) package instant
chocolate pudding mix

1 cup sour cream  *7.4 oz*

½ cup vegetable oil  *3.6 oz*

⅓ cup Kahlúa  *2.2 oz*

¼ cup hot water  *— 1 tsp.*

Grated zest of 2 oranges

1¼ teaspoons ground cinnamon

4 large eggs  *3 eggs + ½ egg*

1 (12-ounce) package semisweet
dark or white chocolate chips,
or a mixture of the two  *11 oz*

*Takes about 10-15 min longer than stated.*

*Used ⅓ cup Crème de Cacao plus 1 tsp liquid coffee. Good!*

1. Grease and flour a 10-inch tube pan or fluted tube mold; set aside. Preheat the oven to 350° (325° for a dark-finish pan).

2. In a large workbowl of a heavy-duty electric mixer, combine the cake mix, pudding mix, sour cream, oil, Kahlúa, water, zest, cinnamon, and eggs on low speed, adding the ingredients one at a time. Beat on medium-high speed for 3 minutes, scraping the bowl often. The batter will be smooth and creamy. Add the chocolate chips and beat until just evenly distributed.

3. Pour the batter into the prepared pan. Bake on the center rack of the oven for 55 to 60 minutes, or until a cake tester inserted into the center comes out clean and the cake springs back when touched lightly. Remove from the oven rack and cool on a wire rack for about 1 hour before turning out of the pan.

*This recipe works better if you put all ingredients except chips into bowl before mixing.*

*6 tsp = 2 TBSP = 1 oz*

*Cake Mix = 16.5 oz now*
*Pudding = 3.4 oz*
*reduce sour cream — by 4 tsp*
*oil - by 2 tsp*
*Kahlua - 1.5 tsp*

# Sweet Brunch Cornmeal Cake

1. Grease the bottom and sides of one 9 by 13-inch baking pan or spray with nonstick vegetable cooking spray; set aside. Preheat the oven to 350° (325° for Pyrex or dark finish pan).

2. In a large workbowl of a heavy-duty electric mixer, combine the dry cake mix and cornbread mix. Add the eggs, oil, sour cream, buttermilk, and water and beat on low speed to combine, 30 seconds. Increase to medium-high speed and beat for 2 minutes, scraping the bowl often. The batter will be smooth and creamy.

3. Scrape the batter into the prepared pan with a rubber spatula. Bake on the center rack of the oven for 40 to 45 minutes, or until a cake tester inserted into the center comes out clean, the top is dry, there are small cracks across it, and it springs back when touched lightly with your finger. Remove from the oven and cool on a wire rack in the pan at least 30 minutes before cutting into oversized squares.

*Makes one 9 by 13-inch cornbread, about 15 servings*

1 (18¼-ounce) package yellow cake mix (such as Duncan Hines Deluxe Yellow Cake)

1 (15-ounce) package corn bread mix (such as Krusteaz Honey Cornbread)

4 large eggs

⅓ cup vegetable oil

½ cup sour cream

1 cup cultured buttermilk

1 cup water

# Butters, Jams, and Fruit and Cheese Spreads

Breakfast is the showplace for homemade spreads for your breads. While we are blessed with an incredible array of store-bought jams, jellies, and preserves, I have found a few really excellent spreads are well worth making at home. Apple butter is a make-at-home must, and fruit curds, made with eggs and butter, are never as good off the shelf. Homemade cheese spreads shine on the breakfast table, as do oven fruit butters. Sweet compound butters—soft butter beaten with some other ingredients—put the finishing touch on toast, muffins, or breakfast rolls.

I like to make jams and butters that use up extra fresh fruit I have around or have been given from a friend's garden, or ones that use dried fruit, which has a concentration of flavor. I look for recipes that are easy to prepare and not too messy. I also search out a flavor that can't be duplicated in commercial preparations.

*From front to back: Chocolate Butter, Tart Dried Cherry Butter, Cranberry-Lime Curd, Whipped Honey Butter, and Small-Batch Fresh Strawberry Jam*

# Apple-Pear Butter

Makes about 2 cups

4 large (about 1 pound) firm tart green apples, peeled, cored, and coarsely chopped

4 to 5 (about 1 pound) firm Bartlett pears, peeled, cored, and coarsely chopped

½ cup apple or pear juice

¼ cup firmly packed light brown sugar, or to taste

2 teaspoons ground cinnamon

¼ teaspoon of ground cardamom

¼ teaspoon of nutmeg

4 tablespoons (½ stick) unsalted butter, cut into pieces

*I used to dine at the restaurant of a friend who created the recipes for the Sonoma Mission Inn when it introduced spa cuisine in the 1980s. His Sunday brunch always had a small bowl of apple butter for the biscuits. The apple butter, which he made the day before, tasted very much like applesauce. A few bites of the thick fruit purée and I was asking for a bigger bowl, one to eat as a side dish. When I found a prototype of his recipe in the Inn cookbook, Spa Food, I was off and cooking my own batch. Here I mix both pears and apples, which is a wonderful combination. I have even been known to throw in a few wayward apricots at times.*

1.  Place the apples and pears in a heavy medium saucepan or Dutch oven with the apple juice, brown sugar, and cinnamon, cardamom, and nutmeg. Bring to a boil over high heat, decrease heat to low, and then simmer, uncovered, until soft, about 30 minutes.

2.  Purée in a food processor, fitted with the metal blade, or with a handheld immersion blender until smooth. Stir in the butter until melted. Transfer to a covered container, such as a spring-top glass jar, cool to room temperature, and store, covered tightly, in the refrigerator for up to 1 month.

# Very Old-Fashioned Prune Butter

*I love anything with prune in it—prune bread, prune Danish, prune-filled cookies, stewed prunes, you name it. Here is a lovely prune spread for toast. The apple cider vinegar, one of my other favorite ingredients, balances the whole mixture and gives it depth. I use natural cider vinegar from the health food store or gourmet supermarket, (one with the "mother"—the starter used to make vinegar—floating around in the bottom), which is quite delicate in taste.*

1. Place the prunes and water in a heavy medium saucepan or Dutch oven. Bring to a boil, then decrease the heat to low, and simmer, uncovered, until very soft, about 30 minutes. Drain the liquid (or drink it; the prune water is delicious), leaving the prunes in the pan.

2. Add the honey, apple cider vinegar, lemon zest, cinnamon, clove, and allspice. Simmer over low heat, stirring occasionally with a large spoon, about 10 minutes; the prunes will become mashed. Transfer to a covered container, such as a springtop glass jar, cool to room temperature, and store, covered tightly, in the refrigerator for up to 3 weeks.

*Makes about 2 cups*

2¼ cups (about 1 pound) pitted prunes

3 cups water

⅓ cup honey

¼ cup apple cider vinegar

Grated zest of ½ lemon

½ teaspoon ground cinnamon

¼ teaspoon ground clove

¼ teaspoon ground allspice

# Tart Dried Cherry Butter (Illustrated on page 140)

*This recipe is somewhat of an extravagance since dried cherries are a bit costly, but sometimes I can't resist indulging.*

Makes about 2 cups

2 large (about ½ pound) firm tart green apples, peeled, cored, and chopped

6 ounces tart dried cherries

1 cup apple-cherry juice

⅓ cup firmly packed light brown sugar

1. Place the apples, cherries, and juice in a heavy medium saucepan or Dutch oven. Bring to a boil, then decrease heat to low, and simmer, uncovered, until the fruit is soft and thick, about 45 minutes. Halfway through cooking, stir in the sugar.

2. Transfer the mixture to a blender or a food processor fitted with the metal blade and process until smooth. Transfer to a covered container, such as a springtop glass jar, cool to room temperature, and store, covered tightly, in the refrigerator for up to 1 month.

# Apricot Butter

Makes about 2¼ cups

3 cups (18 ounces) dried apricots

2½ tablespoons sugar

1 cup water

3 tablespoons brandy

In a small saucepan, combine the apricots, sugar, and water. Bring to a boil, cover, and lower the heat to low. Simmer until soft, about 10 minutes. Add the brandy. Cool slightly to room temperature. Purée the mixture until smooth in a food processor fitted with the metal blade or push through a food mill. Cool to room temperature to use immediately, or store in the refrigerator.

# Fresh Apricot Oven Butter

*My friend Lou Pappas makes scrumptious oven butters, which are just like a thick jam, with no fat and virtually no sweetening. They are fantastic and so delightfully easy to prepare. If you have overripe fruit, this is the perfect place to use it up. The butter is as good on toast as it is swirled in plain yogurt. For a nice variation, substitute fresh pears or fresh plums for the apricots (add 1/4 cup chopped crystallized ginger and a dash of vanilla extract to the pears). I store half of the butter in the freezer. Refrigerated, it should be used within 2 to 3 weeks for optimum flavor.*

*Makes about 3 1/2 cups*

4 long strips orange zest

2 pounds fresh ripe apricots, pitted and coarsely chopped

3 tablespoons honey, or to taste

1. Preheat the oven to 300°.

2. Place the orange zest in a blender or a food processor fitted with the metal blade. Add the apricots and honey and process until smooth.

3. Pour the mixture into a 9 by 13-inch Pyrex or ceramic baking pan. Bake on the center rack of the oven for 1 hour, uncovered, stirring 3 times during baking. The purée will thicken. Remove the pan from the oven and let the purée cool to room temperature. Use a rubber spatula to transfer to a covered container, such as a springtop glass jar, and store, covered tightly, in the refrigerator for up to 3 weeks.

# Chocolate Butter

(Illustrated on page 140)

*This exquisite butter uses the kind of cocoa you would use to make hot chocolate drinks; it is already sweetened. Serve with yeasted or quick breads.*

With a heavy-duty electric mixer on low speed or a food processor fitted with the metal blade, mix the butter and cocoa until smooth. Using a rubber spatula, scrape the butter into a small bowl, or roll into a log shape. Cover with plastic wrap and store in the refrigerator for up to 2 weeks. For easiest spreading, let stand for 30 minutes at room temperature to soften.

Makes ½ cup

8 tablespoons (1 stick) unsalted butter, at room temperature

3 tablespoons sweetened cocoa powder

# Peanut Butter Cream Cheese

*We've all heard about the glories of chocolate paired with peanut butter—but cream cheese and peanut butter? One bite and I guarantee you'll be a convert. You can use other types of nut butters or you can add some chocolate chips or chopped dried fruit; but I like it smooth.*

Using a heavy-duty electric mixer on low speed or a food processor fitted with the metal blade, beat or pulse the cream cheese and peanut butter until smooth. Use a rubber spatula to scrape into a small bowl. Cover with plastic wrap and store in the refrigerator for up to 2 weeks. For easiest spreading, let stand for 20 minutes at room temperature to soften.

Makes about ½ cup

4 ounces cream cheese, at room temperature

3 heaping tablespoons smooth or chunky peanut butter

# Whipped Honey Butter

(Illustrated on page 140)

*My grandmother Nanny Smith used to have a spicy whipped honey butter for me to spread on toast when I visited her. Whenever I make this recipe, I think of her. Since honey is the dominant flavor of this spread, I recommend choosing a light-flavored honey, such as orange blossom, clover, or wildflower.*

Using a heavy-duty electric mixer on medium speed or a food processor fitted with the metal blade, beat or pulse the butter until smooth. Add the fat-free milk (through the feed tube, if using a food processor) while the motor is running, beating or pulsing until fluffy. Slowly add the honey and the flavoring, if using. Scrape with a rubber spatula into a storage bowl with a tight-fitting lid and refrigerate for up to 2 weeks. For easiest spreading, let stand for 30 minutes at room temperature to soften.

Makes 2 cups

8 tablespoons (1 stick) unsalted butter, at room temperature

1 tablespoon fat-free milk

2/3 cup honey

1 teaspoon ground cinnamon or vanilla powder, optional

# Ginger Butter

*Sweet, spicy-hot, and creamy, this butter is great on oatmeal scones (page 18) or plain waffles.*

With the motor of a food processor fitted with the metal blade running, drop the pieces of ginger through the feed tube to grind it up. Stop the machine and add the butter, and then process until smooth and the ginger is evenly distributed. Using a rubber spatula, scrape the butter into a small bowl, or roll into a log shape. Cover with plastic wrap and store in the refrigerator for up to 2 weeks. For easiest spreading, let stand for 30 minutes at room temperature to soften.

Makes 1/2 cup

2 tablespoons candied crystallized ginger

8 tablespoons (1 stick) unsalted butter, at room temperature

# Strawberry Butter

Makes 1¼ cups

1 pint strawberries, rinsed and hulled

2 tablespoons sugar, or to taste

2 tablespoons Grand Marnier or freshly squeezed orange juice

Grated zest of 1 orange

12 tablespoons (1½ sticks) unsalted butter, at room temperature

*This is a glamorous fruit butter. It is cooked a bit to intensify the fruit flavor (strawberries have a lot of water) and is better made a day or two ahead to meld the flavors. Try it on toast and Biscuit Muffins (page 10).*

1. Place the strawberries in a blender or a food processor fitted with the metal blade, and purée. If you don't like seeds, press the purée through a fine-mesh sieve. Place the purée in a small saucepan and add the sugar and liqueur or orange juice. Bring to a boil, decrease the heat to low, and simmer, uncovered, until the liquid evaporates, 5 to 8 minutes. Add the zest. Remove from the heat and let cool completely, and then refrigerate until chilled, at least 2 hours.

2. Using a heavy-duty electric mixer on low speed, beat the butter. Slowly add in the chilled strawberry mixture, mixing to combine. Spoon the strawberry butter into a serving dish, cover, and refrigerate for up to 1 week. For easiest spreading, bring to room temperature before serving.

# Cranberry-Lime Curd (Illustrated on page 140)

*Sweet and tangy fruit curds, so popular in the British Isles, can be made from any fruit, not just lemons. This version can be conveniently made year-round since it calls for canned whole cranberry sauce. The fresh limes are a must. Try not to eat this off the spoon; it is so luscious, you'll be tempted. This curd is a natural with English Muffin Batter Bread (page 45), toasted, of course.*

1. Place the cranberry sauce, sugar, lime juice, zest, and eggs in a food processor fitted with the metal blade and process until a thick emulsion is formed, about 20 seconds. While the machine is running, add the melted butter through the feed tube.

2. Pour the mixture into a medium saucepan and cook over medium-low heat, stirring constantly with a wire whisk. Cook until thickened, about 20 minutes. Pour into a springtop glass jar and let stand until cool. Store in the refrigerator for up to 3 weeks.

Makes $1\frac{1}{2}$ cups

1 (16-ounce) can whole cranberry sauce

$\frac{1}{2}$ cup sugar

$\frac{1}{2}$ cup freshly squeezed lime juice

Grated zest of 2 limes

4 large whole eggs

8 tablespoons (1 stick) unsalted butter, melted and cooled

# Apricot-Pineapple Preserves

Makes about 2½ cups

1 (7-ounce) package dried apricots, coarsely chopped

1 (20-ounce) can crushed pineapple in its own juice, drained (reserve juice)

1 cup unsweetened pineapple juice concentrate, thawed

*I am just crazy about this recipe. It is not only quick to prepare, but it tastes ever so good. Add sugar or honey, to taste, if you like, but I think you will find it is quite sweet enough just from the fruit.*

1. Combine the apricots, pineapple juice drained off the canned pineapple, and pineapple juice concentrate in a deep saucepan. Bring the liquid to a boil over high heat, decrease heat to low, and simmer, uncovered, until the apricots are plump and the liquid has evaporated and thickened, 15 to 20 minutes. Add half of the crushed pineapple and stir to combine. Remove from the heat and purée in a blender or in a food processor fitted with the metal blade.

2. Stir the remaining crushed pineapple (you want it slightly chunky) into the hot mixture. Use a rubber spatula to transfer the preserves to a springtop glass jar. Let stand until cool. Store, covered, in the refrigerator for up to 2 months, or spoon into small freezer bags and freeze.

# Small-Batch Fresh Strawberry Jam

*My mom is known for the small-batch strawberry jam that she makes throughout strawberry season. She likes it soft, runny, and intensely flavored with big berries in it. While she makes hers in the microwave, I get a better consistency cooking on the stovetop. Be sure to scald the storage jars (such as French confiture glass jars with plastic lids, quilted jelly jars, or glass-topped jars with wire closures) even though you will be storing the jam in the refrigerator.*

1. Place the berries in a large bowl and coarsely crush them with a potato masher, leaving lots of whole or semi-whole berries. Place in a deep, heavy, nonreactive saucepan. Sprinkle with the pectin. Let stand 10 minutes.

2. Add the lemon juice and sugar and simmer over low heat until the sugar is dissolved, stirring constantly. Increase the heat to medium-high, and bring to a full boil, stirring frequently to avoid scorching on the bottom. Cook, skimming off the white foam with a large metal spoon, for about 15 minutes, or until it has thickened and a spoonful begins to gel when dropped onto a plate that has been chilled for 10 minutes in the freezer. Spoon into storage jars and let stand until cool. Store, covered tightly, in the refrigerator for up to 2 months (if it lasts that long!).

*Makes about 2 cups*

3 pint baskets fresh ripe strawberries, washed, drained, and hulled (about 4½ cups)

1 (1¾- or 2-ounce) box powdered pectin (use the type designed for low amounts of sugar)

1 tablespoon freshly squeezed lemon juice

½ to 1 cup sugar, or to taste

# Pashka Sweet Cheese Spread

Serves 8 to 10

1 cup heavy whipping cream

1 ½ teaspoons pure vanilla extract

2 tablespoons Chambord raspberry liqueur

2 ½ pounds fresh farmer's cheese

4 ounces kefir cheese or cream cheese

1 cup (2 sticks) unsalted butter, at room temperature

¼ cup liquid egg substitute

1 cup superfine sugar

Grated zest of 1 orange and 1 lemon

¼ cup dried currants

¼ cup golden raisins

¼ cup dried cranberries

¼ cup minced dried apricots

¼ cup minced dried pineapple

½ cup slivered blanched almonds, plus ½ cup for decorating side of cake

*Pashka, typically served as a spread for a sweet yeast bread, is one of the most traditional of Greek Orthodox Easter foods. This is the ultimate breakfast cheese spread, really fancy country food. When I was taking a class at Tante Marie's cooking school in the 1970s, we made pashka as a holiday cheese. We sliced off pieces and had it with butter cookies as a dessert. It was love at first bite, and I have been making this fruit- and nut-enriched cheese in some form or another ever since. I use a commercial egg substitute instead of raw eggs. In lieu of a carved, truncated wooden pashka mold, a mesh or metal rounded colander with the capacity of about 2 ½ quarts will do nicely (old-time bakers used a clean clay flowerpot!). A cone-shaped chinois strainer, available in cookware shops, is close to the traditional shape, right down to its planed tip. Serve with slices of Rye and Honey Fruit Bread (page 110).*

1. In the workbowl of a heavy-duty electric mixer fitted with the whisk attachment, place the cream, vanilla, and liqueur. Whip on high speed until soft peaks form. Scrape into a small bowl and set aside.

2. Without washing the workbowl and switching to the paddle attachment, add the farmer's and kefir cheeses and butter. Cream on low speed until fluffy. Add the egg substitute and beat in the sugar on low speed until well combined. Add the whipped cream mixture, zests, dried fruits, and almonds and mix on low speed, just to evenly distribute all the fruits.

3.  Line desired mold (see headnote) with 2 layers of damp cheesecloth, letting the excess hang over the edge. Spoon the cheese mixture into the mold, filling it to the brim. Fold the edges of the cloth over the cheese. Press down gently to pack into the mold. Cover tightly with plastic wrap and place a heavy object, such as an aluminum foil–wrapped brick or large can of tomatoes, on the cheese. Place over a shallow bowl and refrigerate for 24 to 48 hours to drain.

4.  Remove the cheese from the refrigerator and remove the weight. Discard any accumulated liquid. Remove the plastic wrap and peel back the folds of the cheesecloth. To unmold, place a serving plate over the mold and quickly invert. Gently lift off the mold and peel off the cheesecloth. Stud the sides with the almonds. Serve immediately. Store any leftovers, tightly wrapped, in the refrigerator for up to 4 days.

# Breakfast Cream Cheese and Jam

Makes about ½ cup

4 ounces cream cheese, whipped
 soy cream cheese, or kefir cheese,
 at room temperature

2 heaping tablespoons fruit
 preserves, marmalade, or jam
 (choose your flavor)

*I love orange marmalade, plum jam, or boysenberry preserves already mixed into my cream cheese for toast. This ends up tasting like a whole lot more than just the sum of its parts.*

Using a heavy-duty electric mixer on low speed or a food processor fitted with the metal blade, beat or pulse the cream cheese and preserves until smooth. Use a rubber spatula to scrape into a small bowl and cover with plastic wrap. Store in the refrigerator for up to 2 weeks. Let stand 15 minutes at room temperature for easiest spreading.

# Vegetable Cream Cheese

Makes about 2½ cups

1 celery stalk, finely chopped

½ carrot, peeled and finely grated

1 large plum tomato, halved,
 seeded, and diced

3 tablespoons finely chopped
 fresh cucumber

1 to 2 tablespoons minced chives
 or cilantro, or to taste

8 ounces cream cheese, at room
 temperature

½ teaspoon white Worcestershire
 sauce

Dash of Tabasco or liquid drained
 off some salsa

*For those mornings when you don't want something sweet, this fresh vegetable spread is perfect on Bagel Bread toast (page 42).*

Drain the chopped vegetables on a paper towel. Place all of the ingredients in the workbowl of a heavy-duty electric mixer fitted with the paddle attachment. Beat on low speed just until evenly combined. Transfer to a serving dish, cover, and refrigerate until ready to use. Serve on thin slices of fresh or toasted bagel bread.

# Index